A Franchesca Jiménez
con el mayor de los
aprecio,

El Indio Uribe

8 Agosto 2018

# Reflection-Reaction-Action:

# 365 Reflections for a Successful Living

Eladio Uribe

Dominican Republic
2018

Photos: Eladio Uribe©
Cover Design:  Jael Uribe©
Layout and General Design: Jael Uribe
Translation: Aida Josefina Troncoso
Collaborators: Santa Luchy De Camps and Martha de Lebrón
Proofreading: Luis Ernesto Heredia Batista

ISBN-13: 978-9945091861
ISBN-10: 9945091867

Reflection-Reaction-Action:
365 Reflections for a Successful Living

http://facebook.com/reflexionreacionaccion
Email: eladiouribe@icloud.com

# Content

# Sections

Eladio Uribe

To my children:


Elda Carolina (In Memoriam)
Jael Elizabeth
Anely Darissa
Luz Mayrel
Mélary Esther
Vladimir Amaury
Juan Jorge
Juan José
Dariel Alejandro

To my Granddaughter, María Victoria

# Foreword

I t is an honour and a privilege for me to have been chosen by my colleague and friend Eladio Uribe to write the prologue of his book for this English edition.

I met Eladio in Quito (Ecuador), three decades ago, in mid 1988 when we both worked in our respective National Professional Associations (Dominican Republic and Argentina, respectively) on the occasion of the Latin American Congress of the Inter-American Federation of Personnel Administration (FIDAP), today the Inter-American Federation of Human Resource People Management Associations (FIDAGH), one of the four continental associations that make up the World Federation of People Management Associations (WFPMA) together with the Asia Pacific Federation of Human Resource Management (APFHRM), the European Association for People Management (EAPM) an the North American Human Resource Management Association (NAHRMA).

Throughout these years we have worked jointly in national, continental and world congresses. We worked in different positions in these institutions, so in addition to visiting each other in our respective countries we engage in the development of institutional and academic projects related to people management, human capital and human talent.

We have always agreed on the way of thinking and managing in all substantial aspects of the topics in which we have dealt with. Eladio deserves my great respect as a professional and as a human being, and this is, fundamentally, what motivated me to accept the honourable task of writing these lines.

In his book, entitled "Reflection-Reaction-Action: 365 reflections for a successful living", Eladio elaborated on 365 thoughts with the aim of guiding our actions. He organized them in three groups:

Reflection (146, 40%), Reaction (91, 25%) and Action (128, 35%), one for each day of the year.

These thoughts are reflections, meditations, suggestions, guides, aphorisms and, sometimes, sayings that constitute a kaleidoscope of experiences and recommendations for action, I would say, for life.

I would like to highlight the 37 thoughts that impacted me the most, although, of course, all of them are important. I grouped them based on my own criterion and knowing that, as it is the case with all classifications, it is as arbitrary as the mind of the person who makes it.

Thought № 37 encourages us acting well in thought and deed rather than not doing, and that reminds me of Pascal's reflection on the belief in the existence of God when he says that "It is better to believe than not to believe, given the consequences of one over the other".

Thought №154 recommends not being afraid of giving it all and starting over again. Now, I remember another author, Rudyard Kipling, and his famous poem "If" where he recommends not being afraid of risking all our profits even if we lose and have to start over again as many times as necessary, with worn tools without complaining about loss.

Thoughts № 162, № 252 and № 317 remind us that we must always face challenges and that our duty is to overcome them because that is how we grow and excel.

Issues related to the importance of reflection, self-reflection and cultivating the virtue of prudence appear in № 05, № 122, № 207, № 227, № 235, № 236 and № 239.

Thoughts № 305 and № 312 make reference to the strategic principle and recommendation of conduct, "concentration", that is, focus on what really matters. Thoughts № 218 and № 301 made me think of the Greek Areté as they highlight the sense of excellence our actions should have in any aspect of life, either as leaders or peasants, as Hesiod points out.

That is to say, that we must make our best effort in what we do yet setting our priorities (Thought № 96).

A set of reflections including thoughts № 42, № 46, № 170, № 186, № 253 and № 62 has to do with the moral and solidarity obligation of sharing the knowledge we possess with our neighbour, avoiding "intellectual selfishness". I believe that being afraid of expanding our knowledge is typical of individualistic, selfish and unassertive people. Knowledge is the main tool for getting people out of poverty and when we consciously do not share it, we contribute to that condition. If we are afraid of others knowing as much as we do, what we should do is to teach everything we already know and also strive to improve ourselves so as to know more. This is also related to self-confidence, tenacity and perseverance in achieving what we aim for (Thoughts № 335 and № 359), knowing that this involves great effort and leaving our comfort zone.

I purposely kept a group of thoughts for the end of these brief comments, and these are № 3, № 16, № 55, № 82, № 83, № 107, № 125, № 166, № 188, № 193, № 278, and № 293 because in my opinion they are the most important ones. I associate them with the Stoic philosophy -in its second stage of the beginning of our era in Rome- ,especially with what Epictetus said in some of his fragments. The philosopher teaches us that we can control but ourselves and not the world around us, and illustrates this with the death of a close relative, claiming that this is not a fact we can control, but we can control how we feel about it, and that feeling depends on us. In this sense, I understand that there is much of Epictetus in Eladio´s reflections.

Finally, it should be said that this is a book that you could read lightly and quickly but it is worth reading it slowly so as to give yourself the chance to reflect on each and every thought.

I congratulate Eladio on his work.

**CARLOS ALDAO ZAPIOLA**

# Remarks

His reflections go deep inside of me, by the simple way in which, many times, he expresses very deep feelings. He writes with the language of the soul, of the heart and conveys sensations and emotions that touch the most sensitive fibers of whoever reads him, regardless of the degree of education or study he (or) she has. His writings motivate me to take some action, change or shape a behavior, rethink my views and question my assertions. Above all, I love that personal and poetic touch that he gives them. Regardless of what the subject to be treated is, it always adds that stream of humanity and empathy.

Arianne Florián, dominican resident in New York

You may sign as Eladio Uribe, a man who becomes a friend, uncle, teacher, from the very first day you begin to read this book. Any human being has a million things to say, but you can sign them with your actions. He does not just write, but paints hopes in the life of human beings who are breathless even after the pain is over. With short phrases or sentences he writes great and long conversations. With the same argument, he uses any topic of life itself, touching the finer fibers of the soul of the reader (it has happened to me). It is presented to people in such an uncomplicated way that one immediately identifies with it. Lacerated man, but never collapsed, curing himself, he heals the one who is wounded with him. I think the celebrities are not only the dead writers we read, rather they are the ones that are still alive as you, they teach with dignity, not only the reader, but it is understood that the writer knows that he knows a lot. It makes you think, act; it's like that double-edged sword that shines any way you look at it. That's his pencil, straight, no names, but with skirts, ties, backpacks, for everyone. Very proud to have not only read, but to receive permission to touch his soul ...

Santa Luchy De Camps, Psychiatry Professional, USA

I am one of the many who have been pleasantly trapped in the reflections that Eladio Uribe gives us every day, thanks to his steeped professional and human experience. These reflections move and prepare us to have the attitude to come out triumphant in a wide variety of situations, being them discrete or disruptive changes, of high level of ambiguity, uncertainty or high complexity, which demand a high level of creativity and innovation, in social and in everyday situations, among others.

Manuel González, Dominican Republic

E very daily reflection of my friend Eladio Uribe is full of wisdom and boldness. The wisdom that experience brings to the person who is self-made and who works tirelessly for the common good, the wisdom of the person who learns with an experience that is not always favorable, and the wisdom of someone who knows that the best way to enrich yourself is to share. And the boldness. The audacity of the brave who does not mind swimming against the tide; the audacity of someone who knows what he is saying, and at the same time says what he knows and what he wants, and the audacity that demonstrates that the world belongs to the people that put ethics as the main value. Thanks Eladio. Reading you daily is like being able to bathe every day in your Caribbean Sea, living in Madrid, a European city without sea.

Carlos Hernández, España

T he lessons I received from childhood, both through the example and secular studies, have given me the ability to identify sources that add to my knowledge. When I read writings of people with great intellect like Mr. Eladio Uribe, it is inevitable to enter my brain library to properly interpret the message. Once I get the sense, there is the need to publicly express the effect it creates in me. I am pleased to share my assimilation, because I consider it as a compulsory propagation of the lesson learned.

Mayra Castellanos

# Acknowledgments

The English version of my book, Reflection- Reaction-Action happens 2 years after the Spanish edition, thanks to the insistence of friends from all over who has made this book their main consulting reference. A book is the result of how its readers use it. It could be an awareness instrument or a defense instrument to which we go back frequently whenever we have difficult situations to solve without anyone's help. Wherever I go I meet readers that follow my reflections. Many people tell me how impacting these have become to be in their life. Others, on the other hand, talk about the particular reflection they like the most out of the 365 included in the book. The most audacious go as far as to narrate how they have been able to change others by creating the habit in them of reading the book on a daily basis. A certain teacher from my hometown uses the book as an instrument to reform what he calls mischievous youngsters (crooks) or to help in the development of adult-age people who still behave as children. In short, I have enough motives to be thankful about the results of the publication of the first edition of a book where nothing is left to fate. Every detail is thought out on how to instill a legacy of values, purposes and a sense of happiness in the reader. The facts tell me that this has been accomplished. The actors: readers, transmitters, book sellers, collaborators, followers and distributors who multiply across Latin America, making possible that each day more and more people get hooked up to a reading that is light, of a permanent actuality and a guide to find better ways of living.

With this English edition we only hope to influence people from other regions of the planet, explore new possibilities to consider and to transform the experiences into deliberations in order to come up with new reflections that keep on contributing to change us positively, leaving indelible footprints of excellent achievements, mental liberation, fortitude of purposes, sense of opportunity, respect for diversity and a celebration of life.

We have kept, excepting the natural adaptations, the Spanish edition format, but we came up with a different cover for this English edition. Likewise, it is good to mention that all the pictures included in this edition were taken by me (including the cover photo), and that all of them show a Dominican scenery (with the exception of two of them that were taken in Panama).

I enthusiastically express my enormous gratitude for the timely, precise and decisive collaboration of great friends, friends of forever, who have contributed to make this book a reality. Let me first mention Aida Josefina Troncoso, a great friend, my Human Resources colleague as well as a leadership fellow in the Asociacion Dominicana de Gestion Humana –FIDAGH -. She, without thinking it twice, told me: "I will take care of the translation", and the job was done in record time. After her, another one of my brothers stepped in, Luis Ernesto Heredia Batista. Along the years we have shared very decisive moments and secrets, starting in our adolescence when he was one of my secondary school teachers, and continuing until these days. Our encounters are precious moments that are used to relive our history, to rearrange the present and to rethink the future. Luis, as a goldsmith, dedicated himself to review the translation, making sure that no lapse, punctuation or word got unnoticed lest that distort the meaning that the author intended for each reflection. Many of those who know how competent he is will be glad to know that he has been a fundamental pillar of this new journey.

The collaboration of my dear guiding friend Santa Luchy de Camps, a lady without falsehood, the friend that everyone wish to have, who read the book and gave me her opinions, was really valuable to me. Equally valuable was Martha Lebron's effort in helping Aida Josefine to translate this book.

I hereby also acknowledge the young Dominican artist Emmanuel Geraldo who designed the figure for reflection number 316. It depicts Menpo, the god of the positive mind.

My great friend from many battles, Roberto Santana Sanchez, former Rector of Universidad Autonoma de Santo Domingo, wrote the text for the back cover and made it in such a way that tears rolled down my face. Thank you for everything Roberto, my brother.

Jael Uribe Medina, my eldest daughter, kept on playing a pivotal role for this work, same as she did for the Spanish edition. She designed, reread, diagrammed and made up the composition for this book. She took a very valuable time off from her work as President of the Women Poets International Movement (WPI) and applied herself, like a surgeon, to integrate all the details, keeping embodied my desires and the aspiration of many friends in the book that we gave to the readers' evaluation. I am very proud to have a daughter like her and the result that her effort has meant to me.

I would also like to recognize the worthy and excellent collaboration that was taken upon for the Spanish edition by Salvador Espinal, my teacher, adviser and brother, who wrote the prologue. By the same token, I am also thankful to another great friend, Amarilis García, for her contribution in revising this work, together with the contribution from Arianne Florián, Manuel González, Mayra Castellanos and the Spaniard motivational speaker Carlos Hernandez. My heartfelt thanks go to each one of them.

To reflect on life, feelings, growth, reasoning, participation, development and human behavior have always been of concern to me. Maybe because of my origins, or maybe they are a result of my relations or maybe they come from my profession as a human resources manager; I could not exactly say. The simple truth is that I have always been an optimistic person, a believer in the power of perseverance and, as Nitin Nohria and James Champy would say in their book Ambition: "optimism generates success because it keeps the mind opened to opportunities".

This book is also dedicated to my children for a very simple reason: they are that incandescent breath that keeps me alive. My breath has wrought in its processes of inhalation and exhalation, each one of their aspirations and I walk for them, upright in body and mind, always focused on being an example that does not allow them to lose the approach of a dignified life and without false pretensions.

The reader will continue finding one reflection per page. This way he could open the book wherever he/she wishes and get the appropriate message for the particular moment or situation he/she is in, or instead, he/she could follow the numerical sequence and, like a daily word, have a thought each day during the whole year. Another way to become full of the contents of this book would be to follow the three sections in which the book is divided: Reflection, Reaction, Action. All in all, there are ways for all intentions.

I continue posting my daily thoughts in the social media. Anyone interested could very well follow me through them. Each one of my writings is based in giving the best use to situations that happened to me or to other people because of certain behavior or occurrences in our daily acting, either by ourselves and/or interacting in a group, at work, at home, in entertainment centers, or any other circumstance. In short, each and every moment has become a source of raw material that has allowed for the rise of hundreds of descriptions, of which three hundred and sixty five of them have been reserved for this book.

If a single person, reading what is expressed here, changes behavior, attitudes or habits, and those changes lead him/her to be more successful or to add value to his/her life, I will be deeply pleased to have written the meditations that make up this compendium.

**ELADIO URIBE**

Eladio Uribe

# Reflection

# Sometimes,

you stay thinking about where the door you did not
open takes, and go back to finish the doubt, realizing
that the door is gone, or locked.
The yearning paradise comes to you
through some opportunities.
If you don't take them at the right time,
you'll never find them.

When you can kiss the scents
and embrace the feelings, love blossoms.
Don't let it get away.
The best things happen

# when you make love counts.

# And if you stumble

and fall,
you have the following options: complain, cry and
stay laying down, or lean on the floor,
get up and move forward.
It will always depend on you to stop or to continue,
as well as success or defeat.

# There exist some people
with some stored knowledge
for which they have no use in their daily life
and some knowledge in use
that is completely useless.

# What you have inside
determines your behavior and interests;
it is the result of everything you exhibit.

# Nothing affects more than ignorance.

Nothing creates more loss than the lack of will for learning and there is no one more perverse than the ignorant deceiver.

# The tendency is

almost always
to take the easiest way out,
that which let us invest less energy and resources.
Many times the easiest thing
becomes the most expensive and less durable.
Not always the taste of sweet is healthy.

**08**

Sailing in seas without turbulence, makes the sailboat a ship without emotion or learning.

# Always
## pay attention
## to order,

cleanliness, innovation, and positive thoughts,
because if you get used to the trash,
in a short period of time
you could be so covered by it
that even your thoughts
would wallow in the mud.

**10**

He had become so used to the swamp
that when it dried up, he continued sloshing in it
as if the sludge had not disappeared.

# Routine habits may become more damaging than poison.

# Do you think

you may avoid being blamed
by letting others make difficult decisions for you?
Remember Pilate,
so many centuries later and
he is still considered a great pusillanimous,
as well as a wicked incorrigible.

# What is trust,

but the peace of mind of not having to pursue
the actions of others, while you feel peace
in your soul and judge based only on concrete facts,
not by imagination or prejudice?

I grabbed my cross and like Jesus,
I threw it on my shoulder.
I walked with it to get it to the finish line.
It was not easy, really. It weighted like an elephant,
it had thorns like spikes and the road was long,
difficult; but I didn't give up.
I was constantly encouraging myself to keep on going
and, when my strength ran out, I was laying on
the ground, breathing deep, insisting on commitment
and on starting over.
On one occasion
I wanted to abandon the burden and run elsewhere,
but that phrase I built in my dreams before I left,
forced me to rise:
"Everything is in my mind, it depends on me
and if I do not do it, I will never move ahead".
So now I can write this reflection and say:

# OF COURSE,
# IT CAN BE DONE!

# 1 4

# Fear is a vulgar fool

that we should put in its place.
Sometimes it goes with us and in that case it should
serve as a precaution,
but we must never adopt it or give it a permanent
welcome, but, at the first opportunity, send it to ban-
ishment with absolute determination.

**1 5**

I would be ashamed
that someone
would be ashamed
of me.

**16**

Everything that happens too many times
gets out of control.

# Love In excess

surpasses even madness
and it becomes a mistake or a failure.

Don't ask for what you don't deserve,
not even to God.
Do not shout
when there is no reason and, when there is,
shout only according to the dimension
of the problem, no more.
Do not borrow anything
without prior authorization from the owner, especially
if the owners are all of us.
Do not sharpen the pencil that does not
need to be sharpened because then
you will not be able to write properly.

If you do not like the beach,
do not put your feet in the sand,
you could realize that you were not right.
Don't cough when they're serving the food. They
know you're there and your turn will come.

Good morning, good afternoon and good evening
are not curious phrases of civic books.
They are behaviors of decent people.

# Understood?

# The bad thing would be

for you to realize the importance of the key people in your life when you can no longer count on them.

If not all is like
it seems to be,
then, what is it really?

## 2 0

# How temporary life is!

We must live it with expansive joy so that it covers you, me and also reaches others.
Thus, the chances of being happy will be democratic and each one will be able to opt for what they contain, according to their own disposition.

**2 1**

Hurry your signals and traces;

# someone needs
# to identify you

to give you a farewell speech.
How significant the speech will be
will depend on how long
your footprints may last
without being erased
and your signals without turning off.

**2 2**

Are you one of those who gets bothered
by traffic jams on the road
to the point of losing your temper
and scream at others?
Surely in those conditions
your stress increases so much
that you miss the good music
sounding on your radio,
the smile of the lady
driving the car next to you,
and the sense of the best route to be taken
to get faster to your destination,
among other good situations that surround you.
If so, then,

# why bother
# with those things
# that you are unable
# to change?

**2 3**

# Holistic:

This is how love has to be in order for it to be real and valuable for those involved.

# WATCH OUT:

There are words that hit harder
than several punches in the face.

The circumstance,
The circumstance!
Truly
what is the circumstance
if not the guarantee of knowing
that everything is subject to its action?

And if everything is circumstantial,
what is the need to violate that law
to put on a straitjacket to
the different situations?

Do not violate the natural laws of things,
You could see yourself in the circumstance
of starting all over.

# I have spoken!

**26**

We are all in the dance,
but some dance at a different rhythm
than the one the orchestra is playing ...
even though it does not matter if they are
enjoying themselves.

# We should let everyone dance

to the rhythm that they feel and understand,
as long as it does not affect the larger majorities.

# When a child grows up,

he/she cannot blame his parents for his failures,
but he/she may thank them for his successes.

## Parents,

on the other hand, should let the child make his/
her decisions freely and trust that a good future will
result from them.

# Life is more enjoyable

and relationships are healthier the more we guarantee
the right that others have
to make their own decisions.

**2 8**

# If you're going to compare,

compare yourself and your facts.
It's your habit that determines what you are
and will be, not others.

Wherever you go,
don't try to act like other people.

# Be yourself,

imitations may be good, but they will never be original
performances.

# 30

## Well,

but if you like the routine until fatigue,
no one can prevent that your brain
stop producing dopamine and endorphins,
among other substances capable of transmitting
energy, feeling of fulfillment, love and tenderness.

## To always do the same

is to reduce your emotions
to the minimal expression.

# I hope your gain to be abundant,

your victory to be lasting,
your vitality to be like the oak,
that your perfume attracts without intoxicating,
that your words convince,
for your measures to be always fair,
that your love has the power of multiplication,
but above all, that
whatever your move may be
would contribute to your well-being a
nd the common good.

**32**

That the road
exists is not as important
as the decision to undertake it

until reaching the goal.

If you decide to scratch the wall,
ensure that it is to add value
with what you write or paint.
It is not worth scratching
to increase the garbage in the environment.

# Protests can also be good art.

# The real story

can be hidden by whoever writes it
or narrates it in its own way,
but there will always be a true story
above all falsehoods,
if only in the conscience of those who know it.
Particularly,
when the conscience
acquires quality of expression,
the facts are disclosed, written,
and can be verified.

# Put yourself in my shoes

and you will walk like me.
Put on your shoes and they will adjust,
orient and take the shape of your feet.
Then, with your own shoes
you will mark your footprints and,
if you so desire, you can teach others to walk
with their shoes, not yours.

# The worst thing

is when you think you're right,
without listening to others reasons.

Eladio Uribe

# Today just take a deep breath,

open your heart and your mind, give them your
dreams and projects!
And let it all flow.
Today give space to the relaxation and the connec-
tion of your life with yourself.
Be you and your purposes.

# Three little birds

rushed on a piece of bread
dropped by a child.
It was nice to see them share
with restraint and rationality.
None ate more than the other,
they did not fight each other
and the three were properly satiated.
The most interesting thing was that
there was some leftover bread,
but they, instead of taking it between their paws
and beaks, left it for two other birds who came later
and who also satiated their hunger.

# Tremendous lesson

the birds give to humans!

# Never

will your hunger be better satiated, as when you share food and allow everyone to eat.

# If you keep quiet

about what you feel when you're in possession
of the word, you might hear
what you don't want to hear
when it's someone else's turn.

41

# The entire world

is put at your feet
when you change selfishness by humility
and you accept the others' decisions, regardless of
whether they affect you or not.

**4 2**

# No one

is so smart that has nothing to learn
nor so ignorant that has nothing to teach.

# The advantage

of falling in love with yourself
is that you love without conditions
and over everything else,
and that no one will love you more
than the deep love you give yourself.
By loving yourself,
you put yourself in an advantageous condition
to give and receive love from other people
and to be a center of life in ful.

# There are times

in life
when you have no answers,
even if the questions are the same.

# Never let your friends

feel your absence
when they need attention and solidarity.
If you can't take care of your friends,
you won't be able to serve others either.

# 46

# Can misery be distributed?

How is poverty distributed?
When you give alms you are contributing to poverty;
When you educate,
you are creating the basis for eliminating it.

Followers can be bought when we "give away"

## momentary solutions,

when we give a "bag" with food for a day's worth,
when we give away a few coins;
but we could be incentivizing the end of the story.

A poverty that multiplies
is a suffering majority that grows
and a chaos that becomes gigantic ...
By encouraging the distribution of crumbs
we are not betting on wealth,
but on misery and violence.

# Sharing

with cheerful, wise and experienced people,
with elders who tell about their experiences.
To be among children who enjoy all the details,
to give a pat of gratitude
and see the smile expressed
in the face of an old acquaintance.
How good it is to live in constant learning through
empathy that brings positive beings
and values together!

**48**

# Dreaming of being an elephant

can give you the feeling of being invincible,
but what really turns you into steel
or into ashes is your behavior.

# It's not the same

playing football as playing lotto.

# When you play football

you participate in a team,
you have the possibility to give your opinion,
share with the teammates, sweat to win and laugh
when playing against the adversary.

If you lose, you know there will be more matches
or more tournaments.
In the interim, while waiting for the next game,
you exchange with the members of your team
and with the member of the competing teams,
who may also be your friends.

# When you play lotto

you put hope in question and you usually lose.
You might get excited about the game,
but the chances of winning it are very remote,
as far as Infinity is.
In the end, it is much more exciting
and productive to play football.

When you wake up
with a dream in mind,
all energies conspire in your favor
and all your paths prepare you for its

# fulfillment.

# I have always preferred

loneliness over a bad company,
risk to peace without action,
and the pawned word to the unjustifiable trick.

**5 2**

# Roses,

even when hidden,
allow themselves to be discovered
by their fragrance, because they continue perfuming
the environment, enlarging with colors
and tenderness everything they touch.

# Always

try to be subject, never object.

# Mental old-age

starts when you decide to stop learning, to stop believing, to stop creating, to stop collaborating and allowing nothing to be of interest.

# You decide

who affects you and who teaches you with his/her
behavior.
The same person who now affects you
may give you great learning by simply accepting
him/her as she/he is, or by learning to see him/her
in a different way.
Remember, everything changes when you change.

**56**

# Moments, details.

How good is life
when we fill it with good times
and appreciate each of the details
that make them up!

# Gossip,

unfounded rumor, low blows, discredit,
embezzlement, traps to the innocent,
mockery and tinkering h
ave the same consequences: they cause pain
to whom they are directed,

and provoke or widen the dishonor
of those who cause them.

## 5 8

# Easy come, easy go,

It is more appreciated and more durable that which is obtained on the basis of efforts. This implies sacrifices, daring, persuasion, time, tense situations and putting your capabilities and resources into play.

# Be careful

when giving the hack.
If you hit the wrong stick,
you could lose its future fruits
and its shadow.

**6 0**

# Worry about

making your garden the best vase
and do not waste your time
criticizing your neighbor's garden.

# Improvisation

is good when linked to adventure,
to the emotional expression of joy,
to the visual sense of an illusion or
to the manifestation of the "Me Child".
But when it comes to deciding permanence,
building future, mobilizing resources,
changing jobs or establishing family,
everything must be thought out carefully
and decided conscientiously.

## 62

You get to dream and you

# firmly believe in your dreams.

Boasting solidarity, you breathe faith into others;
you know that everything you want is possible.
Then one day it happens,
suddenly all of what you dreamed about
becomes true and it is about to grant you
what you yearned for.
It's time to be thankful and celebrate.
To receive the kindness of the power of dedication
and the value of a life focused on purposes.

# Harmony

always comes just in time.
If we maintain behaviors based on principles of equality, participation, respect, dignity, synchronicity and
positive attitude, it will be impossible for harmony to
be uncombed or be transformed into denials.

# Life

in harmony is like a fresh spring lap: good life always
flows through its auras.

# Today,

I will also have a better performance.
Not because I aspire to the Oscar as a main actor,
but based on my results, focused on the common
good, on continuous improvement, joy and efficacy in
every purpose.
Today, more positive energies are integrated into this
cause of living better.

# Are you in?

There is no loneliness that cannot be accompanied.
It's all in your mind.

# Do you understand?

# Unforgettable,

because the eternal always remains.

# Indelible.

because deep feelings become stronger over time,
they don't go away.

# Patient,

because it knows how to wait for its process of maturity and splendor.

# Sweet,

because it is such a great and exciting feeling
that it must never hurt;
Just smell, flatter the palate and beautify
the youthful face.
What more can be said of a

# true love?

# It doesn't matter

if the photos are erased;
If you let the memories live on,
your mind will always bring back the images
in the pose you want them to be.

**6 8**

# Some people go away,

but remain at the same time;
Some stay and it's like they're gone;
Others go, come back and go away again;
But the ones who always remain are those whose
performances left traces that marked fates,
opened doors and mutated their hearts to unite
them with yours, building something superior

# Life

regains meaning
and accomplishments get closer
when you forgive and forgive yourself.

# The ice melts,

the rose wilts,
the feeling changes,
the rain stops,
the night transforms,
the film comes to an end

## and life ends.

Everything ends in some way.

# Therefore,

you have to live enjoying every moment
and taking advantage of any opportunity,
because everything can come to an end suddenly
and then, there is no time to start all over again.

# To celebrate

with friends is to weld joy to the colors of life,
is to make a process of achievement from solidarity,
with a sense of pride.
The best friends are like the good brothers:
they are always close to you,
they follow you, they applaud your bad jokes,
they hug you in your misfortunes
and they take you in their arms
to celebrate the victory.
When you do not understand,
they pull your ears or make you cry
with a few words,
until you stop doing stupid things
and start using your brain.
A true friend will never betray you a
nd will always expect
the same behavior from you.

# The speed

at which you go doesn't matter at all
if you don't know where you're heading.

Eladio Uribe

If you keep comparing yourself to others, you'll never be yourself.

**74**

# Today

I observed when the sun came out after the rain
and saw how the green of nature
and life were emphasized in the grasses
and trees of the surroundings.

# From time to time

human beings are in need of a rain
that bathes us in greenery
and brings into us the enthusiasm of living;
However, it is easier when we discover that
the best solutions of motivation
and success are inside of us
waiting to be exploited.

# Slavery

manifests itself in so many ways
that it is better to be careful with exhibitions.
You could be openly displaying your cell bars.

## 76

Sometimes
waiting for a long time is
not a harrowing delay,
but an insurance phase
of permanent victory.

# To the woman

who cries without cause but rightly,
who laughs with the heart and the senses
so that her children know the importance of sincerity
and the fortitude of love.
To the woman who refuses to receive
the percentage share of participation
as if she inspires pity
and prefers to be valued for her merits.
To who was maimed because of an abuser
and who preferred to work more than any man
to provide for her own.
To the one capable of standing on a tribune
and convince, who is captivated with a rose
and does not delude herself with any sophism.
To those who offered their lives
and became martyrs
and without being martyrs
were heroines in the struggle to survive.
To who is still a cocoon and to the one
that has already extended her petals to the sun

## and to them all.

To those deprived of their freedom
and to those who suffer in a hospital.
To the one who jumped to the other side
looking for a better life and to all,
to every one of the faultless, responsible,
dedicated, persevering, helpless, courageous
and brave women of the world,
go my congratulations with a caveat:

# Every day is your day...!

# On many occasions,

one seeks to impose on others lessons
that one must first apply upon oneself.

It's not just what you think;
it's also what you feel.
It's not just what you feel;
it's also what you say.
It's not just what you say;
it's also what you do.
It's not just what you do;
it's also what you do it for.
It is an integral circle.

# Nothing in your thoughts,

behavior and decisions is isolated.

# Making decisions

As long as you have the fever,
everything will seem fine because
you'll act like a blind man,
but when you calm down
and come back to your senses,
you will realize of your mistake,
but it will probably be too late to amend it.

# Never plant seeds

if you are not sure they will grow, or invest in land
without first checking the quality of the soil.
Do not buy fertilizer
without seeing the expiration date.
In terms of investment,
anything that cannot be verified,
threatens to be a farce.
When you sow knowing your seeds and your land,
you will know beforehand the quality
of the expected product and ensure a good harvest.

What do you do when you wake up every day?
Do you turn off the alarm,
turn to the other side
and try to keep sleeping?
Do you start complaining about having to work?
Do you curse your boss?
Do you thank your God for the new day
and put a smile of satisfaction saying:
How good it is to see a new dawn!?
It's all in your mind and it starts
from the moment
you wake up.

If what you say and do is negative
from the moment you start,
you will probably have a bad day,
full of insignificant results and you
will be incapable of laughing and growing.
Why don't you start your actions
from the next dawn on by being thankful,
by putting mind and heart
into achieving growth results?

# Try it!

You will lose nothing, but you will gain joy,
health, outcomes in pursuit of goals,
family satisfaction, respect and growth.

# Sometimes you know everything

without having any contact with others.
You feel as if you are flying
and looking at the panorama from above,
with actors and scenarios included.
You remove and put pieces that end up
composing something important for you.
You travel to places where you always wanted to be,
without moving from your seat
and solve problems that seemed impossible.
When that happens, you are exercising the power
of your mind, you are correlating that power
with your dreams and finding valid answers to the
situations and goals that you have ahead.
It is called synchronicity;
But it is not a problem of name, but
of using well your most precious resource: yourself.
When you learn to manage your mind
and permanently develop the power that is in it,
you put yourself in the position of reaching any goal
regardless of size, complexity, time,
resources or competitors.

84

# A good communicator

knows how to distinguish very well
between chatting, sending an email,
talking by teleconferencing,
making a phone call
or talking face-to-face with the receiver.
Each means of communication
has its rules and although
electronic messaging grows
and changes life, it can never replace
the delight of seeing and touching in person.

# Does love

put up
with everything?

No. Love that tolerates everything is martyrdom.
Does love allow everything?
No. Love that allows it all is weakness.
So, what is love?

Love is recognition, sharing, deciding in duet, trust,
patience and knowledge.
It is an expression of desires and freedom of speech.
Love is a luxury when it is refreshed, forgiveness
when it is sincere, a wait when it is believed and an
expression when it is released. Nothing is worse than
the cowardly love,
the one who learns to create doubts
on imaginary basis.
Nothing compares to the centered love,
the one that is emphasized in the actors
nd produces shared satisfactions.

# There are loves

that die before they begin.
There are those which start and do not end and
some that reach halfway.
Others end and continue to act
as if it did not happen and others
which keep on going by who knows what reason.
We also have those that keep renewing themselves
and always seem new.

The important thing will always be to be satisfied
with what we give and at all times be aware
that we are what we do for ourselves and for others.

# You have in your hands

the most powerful resource
a person could have: your power of choice.
When you choose the least bad,
you're committing a blunder.
The less bad will always be bad
with a good chance of getting worse.
The power of your choice cannot be given away
for unsafe adventures.
It seeks to guarantee your choice
in terms of change, innovation and self-improvement.
Make always sure to choose what will produce
or who will bring about effective actions
for the benefit of all.

# Simple math:

## If you multiply,
you increase what you have.

## If you divide
you share.

## If you subtract
you take away.

## If you add
you add up.

Always be clear of what you want to show with your performances and do not forget that what you do for others also reverts to you.

# Today
# I just want to tell you:

Dream,
believe in your dreams
and do everything you need to do in a completely
and shared way to reach them
and do not allow anyone
to take them away from you.

# What do you know about yourself?

How well do you know yourself?
Excellent!
So, answer the following question:
What is your life's purpose?
What can be expected of you in the next five years?
What do you do when you are questioned?
Do you look for a guilty one, get annoyed
or tell the truth?
When you're afraid, how do you behave?
When was the last time you reviewed
the execution plan for your life purpose?
If you can answer these questions honestly,
congratulations!
If not, take it easy.
Start by discovering who you really are
and then decide how far you want to go.

**91**

# Do not leave
# without effect

the tenderness expressed with a touch.
Do not have the meaning of life go away
without knowing it first.
Do not encourage the abuse
that leaves you without receiving the magic touch
of the smile.
Do not violate the right of others
to prevent the imposing character
of your harmful follies.
Do not trip crudely with the harsh reality
because then you would have left to immaturity
the fever of your decisions.

# Listen to music

whenever you can.
The power of music is magical
because it elevates the spirit,
tunes the senses, appeases the discomfort,
makes the smile flourish, lubricates the heart,
increases the desire to love, forces you to sing
and erases the insignificant.

# Today I just want
# to laugh

at myself, at life,
at each and everyone, at boldness and clumsiness,
at efficiency, at everything and especially at me.
I want to laugh at those believed themselves
to be intelligent and at the humble intelligent.
I believe I already said it all:
today I just want to laugh.

# UBUNTU

In Xhosa culture it means
"I am because we are".
No message can be better in today's world
where individualism, egomania
and a sense of belonging cover us
like a thick covering.
We must return to our origin
and learn that way of living in community,
teamwork and service.
It would be like regaining freedom,
increasing productivity, improving results,
and increasing the benefits for all.

# Now is the time

to learn how to erase
and therefore unlearn what is vain,
wrong, flawed, and meaningless.
Time of emotional intelligence,
time to put a STOP sign
and undertake new ways.

**96**

# One day

my nephew realized that
my father was not seeing well
and sounded the voice of alarm.
When I took him to the ophthalmologist,
it was late.
The doctor diagnosed him
with an aggressive glaucoma
and a few years later
my father was completely blind.
The lack of prevention
and a neglect that became chronic
prevented him from seeing his grandchildren
and great-grandchildren.
Many people stop paying attention
to the most important things on an everyday basis,
to what should be a priority,
to things that,
if they fail, can create difficult situations
as happened to my father.
Remember Stephen Covey's premise:

# "First thing first"

and success will always come timely in your life.

# Happiness

is on the way;
its route is time.
The guide to feel it is the mind,
the driver: the heart.
A beautiful way of expressing it: the joy.
The arrival to the goal is victory.
If you don't enjoy the road,
you'll arrive tired to the finish line
and you won't be able to celebrate
the victory.

.

# 98

# Sunset

is not the arrival of darkness,
but the transformation of light
to make more noticeable
the different colors of life.

Eladio Uribe

Don't swallow your tears.
Let them express
themselves on your face
with sorrow
and lamentations;
But don't let them stay
forever with you.

Why are you trying
to close the doors when they're opening it?
Why do you seek to hide the sun
when it is placing its rays on your smile?
Why do you say no,
when your heart accelerates
on its way to the yes?
Why can't you appreciate the subtle detail of the
process that love shows you?
Why don't you stop your footsteps
and collect the scattered graces
evaporated in the wind?

# Maybe it's time

to check everything and change...

**101**

In the silence of the sunflowers,
the butterflies also get mute.
It is that if the breeze stops
from shaking our tiredness,
the voice is exhausted;
we lose faith and die of pain.
Because of it,

# life continues efficiently

when we all blow against the drowsiness
and drive away with sounds the threats
of the premeditated silence.

# The value of a hug:

the embrace places solidarity in the flesh,
connects hearts and spreads feelings of love.
A hug eliminates the heartaches;
it makes you forget quarrels and provides the confidence needed to start over.
It's amazing how the hug,
even when it seems to be given under hypocrisy,
changes the way you think and feel
for better routes of hope.

When the avenues of solidarity close down,
the world will begin its definitive decline and

# love shall perish.

Solidarity is a shelter that covers from the cold
in the painful situations of life;
it is a fundamental branch of friendship,
a song of sensibility and a force that
recharges the batteries of the suffering one.
To be worthy of solidarity
is like receiving the strength of a balm
that allows you to continue breathing,
despite a strong nasal congestion.

# Do not let

the black cloud of desolation
cover you without appealing to the bright light
of your inner fire.

Have you ever felt that your shadow is upside down?

# If it happened to you

it's because you're feeling so stormy,
that even your shadow turns.
Sit alone by yourself in a quiet
and comfortable place, take a deep breath
and reflect on your situation.
You will find inside of you the causes
and the solutions.

# When you abandon what you cherish for

what surprises you, it is immaturity.
When you persist in the error
knowing the consequences, it is an exaggerated risk.
When you can't choose what you really want
among many options, it is uncertainty.
When you follow your heart and your senses,
you are in sync with your purposes.

# For me

the relationship between knowledge and growth
is the action that justifies the last.
If there is no action that shows achievements
in value added to the players,
the collaborators and the organizations
where they operate, there is no growth.
A role that shows ownership is not worth
if you cannot execute the practice of the knowledge
that leads to growth.

# 108

# I have never seen lasting welfare

in people who live bragging or
wanting to pretend what in reality they are not.
Sooner or later that life
of insignificant exhibitionism goes to the cliff.
Humility and respect for others
will always be the true rules
of durability and glory.

# One should not owe to women or to cemeteries:

they always come to collect
when you least expect it.
Men cannot be given choices:
they never decide on one,
they always want to choose them all,
just to see what happens...

# Sometimes I want to scratch the walls,

have claws to climb through the air
and walk to the solemn spaces of the aurora, taking
a leap towards the infinite emptiness
and embrace without constancy of gaze all dreams. I
would also want to meander
in the crystals of the past and through their lights
transform the boundaries of their channels,
creating a noble future, different,
full of love and sensations.

If there were no good communists,
Engels would not have done his research
on the origin of man and state.
If there were no good capitalists,
the world would not have had the great advances
and discoveries that exist today.
If religion did not have its goodness,
in spite of the Crusades, there would be no talk of
Martin Luther, nor would there have been
a renovator named Francisco.
If the politicians were all corrupted,
José Martí, Abraham Lincoln, Juan Pablo Duarte and
Olof Palme would not have existed.
If we were all corrupt as some people preach,
then what was the role of Juan Bosch
in the Dominican Society,
or Nelson Mandela in South Africa,
or so many men and women
who have honored their organizations? In the end,
what matters is to emphasize that in all areas
and sectors, there are geniuses and mediocre,
good and bad, corrupt and corrupting individuals.
Despite that, the good are still a majority,
and yes, we can build a world where good,
honest, responsible and humane majority,
integrated in all sectors, guide humanity,
making it reborn in a life of

# love and peace.

**1 1 2**

# Build bridges

and hug in the middle of the bridge
those on the other side, cross with them in a hubbub
to celebrate unity and then build new bridges.
There is nothing more important than building bridges
that integrate instead of having to climb
dividing walls.

# Sacrifice

must be an added value to the expected results.
If you want to achieve goals,
but you are not willing to face the risks involved,
your results will be negligible or negative.

# Never remain quiet if you disagree,

if you have another version or position,
or if irregular things are being done in your name
or other people's names.
Remaining silent, more than making you
an accomplice makes you an actor of them.

# Ridiculousness

is like a bad movie.
One tries to get it, over and over,
but there is no way to give it
any favorable mark.

# Most conflicts

arise when one of the parties
breaks the agreements.
It is the duty of honorable people to take on
the commitments and to minimize conflicts.

# A victory

without support from a team
or a group of people
is like a king without a crown.
The world of individual results,
without participation or shared benefits,
must be banished from our behavior,
if we want to be truly successful.

**1 1 8**

# Your future

depends on your habits.
That's why you need to continually review them
and make the necessary changes to achieve
the goals in the most effective way.

# When you undertake a conscious path

of where you want to go,
all the obstacles you find will be exercises
to fully enjoy the success of arriving.

# Do not keep on trying

to justify what does not make sense because then
you would have created a boomerang.

# Don't you believe anyone?

Do you think everyone else needs to change,
but that you're perfect?
Go ahead, your way of thinking is right,
but when you start colliding
and come to the realization
that nothing goes as you believe,

## then stop,

review your plan of objectives,
compare it with your road chart
and analyze your supporters' role.
Maybe then you'll learn that without the others,
you couldn't even get to the bathroom.

**1 2 2**

# ¿Yes or No?

It depends.
Neither the yes is always positive nor the not always
negative. It all depends on where it comes from or
what the question is.
Don't always say yes,
and don't be afraid to say no.

# Just think about it!

Don't carry with you what you're not going to need.
For each place there are different equipment,
materials and feelings.

# You'll never need hate,

grudges or resentments,
but you'll always have to bring love
and the capacity to give it.

**1 2 4**

# No autumn

is better than winter or vice versa,
they are only different seasons.

# Perseverance

is the vital force
that allows us to overcome all difficulties
and achieve goals.

**1 2 6**

# A Rose is a rose,

even if it is withered.
It deserves care and that we enjoy its scent.
A human being has that quality no matter the size,
age, color, religion, or social status.
Respecting and loving
him/her represents the stellar definition of life.

# Being happy

is a condition, an attitude.
It is spirit, nature and action.
There will be days when everything seems to fall,
but if there is a foundation,
nothing will fall, everything will rise above your senses
and you will be happy.
Do not let anyone
change your sense of good living,
not even yourself.

**128**

Today is a day to give
the best of me,
to express my ideas,
to serve, to change
and to be better.

# What is wrong,

like misused words,
it is even noticed by a blind man.
If you do not want your actions to punish you,
try to act correctly.

# Sometimes,

you have to stay quiet and just listen.
Sometimes, you have to dry swallow and not cry.
Sometimes it is better to let the other triumph and

## applaud, not envy.

Sometimes, life presents those dilemmas to us
and it is better to let go.

# When you have

your values and aspirations clear,
you neither buy everything that is being sold to you,
nor you accept
everything offered to you

# A good team

is the one that achieves the best results,
no matter the situations
that it has to face

Everything that happens in the universe
and everything we think or do,
affects us all for good or for bad.
That's why, if we want a better world,

# it's better

that we act well
in thought and in action.

**134**

In the lowest graves
there may be the highest stories.

# It's of cowards to

kick the one who is lying
and it is for the wise to reach out to the needy.

# Wherever you go,

my dear Mandela,
you will always have crowds who adore you.
You are already a part of History
and glory, forever.

# No fear
# is so big

that cannot be eliminated.
No peace is so small
that is not needed.
No love can be so hidden
that cannot be expressed.
No forgiveness is so expensive
that cannot be given.
No love is so small
that does not leave traces.

# Love persist,

even if it hurts,
although it seems
that you cannot reach it

# One attracts to one's life

what one wants this to be.
Your thoughts must express what you aspire
and not what you complain about.

# Life is an adventure in which just the most persevering succeed.

# It costs a lot

to be different.

There are many people
for which it is strange that one
does not follow traditional rules of behavior,
like choosing the "least bad",
forgiving the poorly done,
meeting with wrongdoing people
or accepting handouts to maneuver on their behalf;
but despite the obstacles,
to be correctly different
will always be a victory
with significant profits.

**141**

# Today,

I want to have the greatest aptitude to be effective
in the accomplishment of everything I undertake,
the best of attitudes
to render quality services,
but above all
I want to share the results with others.

# There are 50%

and even 25% of people,
means and resources that
solve 100% of your problems.
There are people, means and resources that,
even being at 100%,
are not enough for even
a 25% of the solutions.

# 143

# There's nothing better

than always being available
for someone who needs you.

Sometimes,

# it is so terrible

the fear
of our own decisions
that we see big ghosts
where there is only praise,
good wishes and love.

If we all kiss the earth at the same time,
would it become more fertile?
Or is it true that those with bad energies
have so much power
that even kissing it would pollute it?

# No,

good is as big as we want it to be,
we only need to believe in it firmly,
feel it in our hearts.
With it, evil will begin to die.

**146**

I'd like to leave this ship
full of ballasts and impossibilities.
I would like to leave it,
even take my footprints with me
and not leave any traces of me,
to mess up the irresponsible people
who fight and mess up everything
so that the others have less
and that they have more of what belongs to us all.
To kick the foolishness
and wastefulness every step of the way,
to rebuild everything in other environments

# and take a leap, now!
I'm just missing you
and I'm not leaving without you,
because alone, I couldn't.

# Reaction

# Many people

live advising others
how to solve their different situations,
forgetting that they themselves,
with similar difficulties,
have not put into practice
their excellent recommendations.

**148**

They penetrate through the eardrums of power,
consume the honey left by
the rich collectors of nectar,
they take to walk the airs of their authority
and tread, without being perturbed,
the claws of those who try to defend themselves.
They are not concerned about what will be said
or where the defeated fall.

# They don't even care about

who their competitors are.
After all, the first thing is to be and by being,
they are receiving the demons
that elevate their egos.
They do not think of withdrawing,
even if their chin touches the ground
and discredit covers them in shame.
There are a lot of Latin American politicians
among them and also traffickers of misery,
whose moral turpitude is well known,
from other backgrounds.

# Exhibitionists

are like glass objects: they can't fall.
They are mistaken the more they speak
and almost always,
they are discovered by the bustle they produce
when pretending to be original.

# Watch Out!

Take care of the structure.
If you don't have the correct dimensions
and the right balance,
it could go down with serious consequences.
This applies not only to physical security
as well as construction,
but also to the human area,
emotional and physical.

# A careless heart

or a mind unable to think rationally
leads to failure or death.
It is best to secure both structures
with adequate reviews,
studies and maintenances,
keeping in mind that it will always be valuable
to get professional help for those issues in which
we are not experts.

# I have

a valve connected to life's positive energy and it,
at the rendezvous point with my body,
has an "antinegative".
This is a little device responsible for letting go through
only that which vitalizes my senses with productive
and happy solutions.
Do you have yours?

# It's free.

# It doesn't matter

if it does not hurt you when you see
a child begging in the street.
It does not matter either if the death
of a child for lack of attention does not move you
to take any action.
What's going to hurt you i
s when it is your turn and nobody cares.

(In tribute to Emil Martin Niemöller).

# Beware,

of the one who,
on many occasions, speaks incessantly
or stops for just a bit.
This is an insecure and fearful person
who is afraid of his own acts
or conceals things he knows or is simply taken
as a "Mad Rooster".
Learn to give your opinion
only when necessary
and when you recognize
that you will make a contribution to improve,
solve, orient or get out of a situation.
If you are going to abound about
what we already know,
just by saying: "I agree ..."
should be enough.

Don't be afraid to give away everything and start over. The one who gives without conditions receives in abundance and the more he/she gives, the more he/she receives.

# Mental blindness

is mediocrity at its worst.
Those people who, based on religious, political,
sports, cultural elements, etc.,
try to impose, no matter what,
their criteria of action on others,
according to their particular beliefs or fanaticisms,
should learn that others have beliefs
that are often divergent,
but they have the same right to express them.

# I have never understood

why so many people, after using the bathrooms,
do not wash their hands.
I observe this more frequently at airports,
when I travel.
Is it that at their home
the water is scarce and
they were not taught the importance of hygiene?
I do not know,
(my apologies to those friends who do not do it),
but all researches talk about
the importance of hygiene,
not only not to pollute,
but also for our well being.

# Never again,

worthless tears,
companions who do not practice honesty
or who would sell even God to justify their outrages,
paths that cannot be walked
or non cutting edges.
Never again, crowns with thorns,
or two-legged dogs,
or legal adjustments that favor the rapist.

# Never again,

the rejection of people because of their color
or the exchanging of misery for bags.
Never again,
more decisions without the participation
of the majorities or without the minorities.
I'm sorry;
I dreamt that it was possible.

# Amen.

**158**

I didn't feel the last earthquake,
but in the different areas of our everyday life

# there are worse earthquakes

that constantly rumble and force us to keep watch,
so as not to fall flat on our faces.

**159**

# There are people

whose performance
is more than deserving of a good "insult".
The problem is that if you do, you put yourself at the
same level as the people you are directing it to.

**160**

# Wickedness

covers those who are not based on values
and are always seeking to benefit from all situations,
regardless of others rights.

# The noise

of boisterous people's is different
from the noise of the cart loaded with products
and that of the ungreased wheels;
it is distinguishable from a distance
because it reveals the mental emptiness
of its producers.

I do not conceive life

# without challenges

that some call problems, difficulties,
nuisances or misfortunes.
The challenges are the best opportunities for learning,
for personal development,
satisfaction and achievement.
Without challenges
you would not force yourself to be better,
you would not set higher goals for yourself
or even be capable of surpassing the hurdles,
cross bridges and fly.

# He was such a son of a bitch;

but such a son of a bitch,
that his fingerprints were all over the place
and his scent was breathed no matter
where you would place yourself.
No one could get rid of him;
they all hated his proceeding.
As nobody ever stopped him,
he kept imposing his rules
and transforming the details in his own way
until he made the mistake of believing that
he was above good and evil.
Then, since he was not called Love
or since he did not lavish love on anyone,
he became ill by the disorder he himself had created
and died for lack of hugs.

**164**

# He was so stubborn,

but so stubborn that
from so much banging himself against the wall,
instead of recognizing his mistakes,
he ended up splitting his head in two halves.
Someone like that urgently needs to work
on his emotions; otherwise,
it could happen that...

# Do not barter with someone else's property.

If that's not robbery,
there are a lot of possibilities
that it will get you into jail
or at least or you to be sent to some
theoretical-practical classes on ethics.

**166**

That Jesus,
being at a wedding in Cana of Galilee,
had turned water into wine,
does not give you the power to believe
that you can drink all the booze in the world
without nothing happening to you.

# Remember:

Exaggerations are the match
that ignites the disaster.

# Any profession
# is a disaster

if it has out of control offers
undefined paths,
dull goals, a non existant coach
or someone who misleads .

.

**168**

It seems nonsensical to me
to pretend feeling what we do not feel
in order to appear courteous
and disciplined to people who we do not need.
It's like buying in a store
where the clerk and cashier are boring and insolent
and you put up with them with a smile.

# Noooo,

being happy also has rules
against hypocrisy.

# When everything

seems futile,
the emptiness of inefficiency arrives.

(Regarding the death of Robin Williams).

If you try to clean someone else's corners
having yours dirty and battered,
you will be dealing with shame
and unhappiness because

# we cannot give
# what we do not have.

# 171

## Sometimes we must achieve,

in any way possible,
for the tongue to become very heavy
so that it is impossible to move it and
the mouth keeps absolute silence,
and moderation takes hold of all our senses,
including the common one.

# The undecided,

are those who always take more
and more time to make a decision,
they are never willing to take risks
and are afraid of even their own shadow.
They end up improvising out of desperation
and, logically, become losers.

# Are you a good or bad news carrier?

Why is it that some people specialize in bad omens
and only talk about misfortunes,
outrages and negative futures?
Do not let yourself be infected
by those soothsayers of evil,
get away from them
and prevent their winds
from blowing on you.

# Experience,

that crazy trip to the past,
often only serves those who want to claim benefits
for which they are not able to compete.
So when the time comes for you to use
such resource, which honestly is something valid,
you must first ensure that your capacities
and attitudes are in present tense with a high poten-
tial for change and good for the future.
Experience is not worth if you can't add value
to what you do.

## I have spoken.

# Daring

is a resource that
the wise knows how to use very well,
because even to be daring,
one must not only have courage
and consciousness,
but also respect for our fellow men.

I have never understood
that about the female quota.
I know that there are injustices,
violations of rights,
discrimination and other atrocities,
but that is not resolved with shared participation
as a rule, but with change of conceptions
and promoting a justice system that values
and encourages equality.
But not a quota.
The only quota that must exist
is that every man or woman will earn the places

# they aspire for
# on their own merits.

If you mock them
when they are absent,
what can I expect from you when I leave?
However,

# I don't care what you can say about me

when I am absent,
but you should be worried about what
you're representing when you talk.

They spend their lives aspiring to positions
they do not know how to handle,
to do things they do know
and that only benefit their pals in their surroundings.
Those who want everything for themselves,
at the expense of others,

# always end up with nothing.

When it's not because they waste it, it's because
they lose it or it is taken away from them.
Extreme ambition is bad company
and the people of that attitude
are called greedy or hoarders.

# How is abuse erased?

When is abuse greater?
When it is constantly received from another person
or when those involved mistreat each other
whenever they can?
There is no deserved abuse;
it is not a punishment,
it is an abuse.
All abuse is incorrect,
a violator of rights and must be rejected.

Two individuals are needed for a fight.
If you don't want to get to the point of aggression
because you are well aware of the consequences,

# appeal to your emotional intelligence

avoiding sterile and aggressive discussions,
clashes while having a drink
and the threats of using a gun
or other instruments, including the fists.
Learning to end something when you are
in possession of mental and emotional control
will always be the proper way
of being rational and effective.

# 181

## Sometimes good eating is bad eating.

You have found the food very tasty
thanks to the great combination of seasonings,
meat fat or junk food
that you ingest without control,
but among too many combinations,
you also taste bad cholesterol,
high blood pressure and harmful fatness.
For this reason it is better to be prudent
in the quantity, to go for a healthy quality
and to manage your food schedules with discipline
before having to withstand
the admonishments of the Doctor
and the threat of a dangerous heart attack.

# I always heard

and read that when calling someone
it is best to start with his/her name
and then make the request
or deliver the message,
but I never thought it was really important
until I heard:
"-Eladio, could you please help me
with something?"
When I heard my name and the question
as to whether I could,
I immediately put myself at the service
of the one who had requested me.
The power of paying attention
and the willingness to contribute
will always be much more effective and fast,
when first you distinguish me by who I am
and then you ask me if I can.

**183**

It's not "fashionable" to be punctual.

# It's a commitment,

a practice for yourself and an incredible
way to be a successful person.
Responsibility with the time of others
guarantees you credibility.
Responsibility with your time guarantees
you emotional stability and moral condition.

# I lend you my company,

so that you go to every place desired by you
and express yourself as you always wanted.
I lend you my applause, to support you
by uttering the dream words.
I lend you my efforts, because all sacrifice for you
will be well taken advantage of.
I lend you my ability to think,
so that if at any time you forget to dream you can
regain the illusions and start again.
I lend you what I am, because a lot of it,
I owe to you and I know that you will give it the
most convenient use.
In short, as always, I know your needs
and special moments.
So, here I am my friend,
for whatever you require of me.

# Don't dislike anyone

for the way she/he is, her/his skin color,
her/his nationality, religion or way of dressing!
Every human being has its own personality.
If you're going to judge someone,
do it for his/her behavior,
not for what he/she is or for how he/she is.

# Don't let anyone forget you

for your lack of action.
No matter what happens
and how it happens always give the best of you
in whatever it is you are asked to do.
Always practice how to get things well done
and when the time comes, go with everything
and show that your dedication
and commitment are not inventions,
but constancy of purposes.

# Don't give your opinion,

not even in social networks,
about what you don't know properly
nor display what you cannot justify.
Someone might call you to account
and you'll complicate yourself
with false explanations.

If you don't allow the mango to ripen,
you'll never taste the best flavor of that fruit.
Many people go from frustration to frustration,
because their desperation
does not allow them to wait
for the natural course of events
that must be given to the processes
to materialize properly.

# Despair is the mother and lady of failure.

# That your medicine is good

does not mean that it can cure all ailments
and much less that it works for all people.
To each one according to their makeup
and the diagnosis.

# There are daring

that are well worth tackling.
What is not right is to go over
and beyond the challenge.

191

What is your price,
how far does your willingness to sell yourself go?
Who can buy you?
Would you dare to give in
to a delicate situation depending on
the price tag they put on it?
Do you let yourself be guided by anyone
who appears in your path making offers to you?

# Are you capable
# of saying no

when the offer does not coincide
with your values and feelings?
It's up to you. Your integrity a
nd the strength of your values
determine who you are.

If you think you have more than you need,
you exaggerate.

# Remember,

everything that's left over can annoy and weight.
If you want to lack everything, then despair.
This way you'll look for crazy solutions
and never get the result you hope for.
Avoiding exaggeration and despair
is when we demonstrate our willingness
to be someone who is measured,
focused on results, a team player, always
open to change and who respects diversity.

Do you know the difference
between the aggression of the wolf
and your capacity to explode in any situation?
It is that you're in control.
The wolf acts by impulse,

# you can act
# with rationality.

Every time you act like a wolf
and not as a rational being,
the explosion will be more painful
and could become your final act.

**194**

# Could we say

that one can trust those people
who speak more than they listen to,
never express what they think
and are always blaming the other?

# To those anonymous heroes,

to those men and women who gave up their
freedom to provide for their children and nephews.
To those who, in spite of being illiterate,
became adults before they could live their youth
and were great entrepreneurs.
To the countless men and women who learned to
move among the rats to cross the finish line
and never tainted their honor.
To those who do not appear in the press
and yet live each day perfecting the art of survival
or doing work worthy of a front page in the news.
To those who between mockery
and ignorance are able to fulfill their dreams and
demonstrate the importance of perseverance.
To those who do not abuse the opposite sex,
nor allow to be mistreated.
To them all go these reflections
which are also a tribute to the woman
who raised me and taught me how to live:
Luz María Suero Piñeyro.

## 196

We can't all be leaders.
Leadership implies a high level of discipline,
empathy, concentration on the principles,
knowledge of the idiosyncrasies
and interests of the followers
and the channeling of positive energies.
The leadership of our time
must also be obtained on the basis of honesty,
sense of service and shared participation.
Not everyone can be a leader;
Being a leader is more than being smart;
it is more than being active
and more than having many titles.
Leadership is unity,
always finding satisfactory solutions
and bringing your flock to a safe harbor.
And above all, leadership is conquered.

# Can you be one?

# I am that
# mother country

waiting for you every day to get ahead
and contribute to the welfare of all.
I am a bunch of needs
that all my children must fill up.
I am your name, your representation,
your flag and the end of all your aspirations.
Don't forget to have behaviors that honor me.

# Long live the
# Motherland!

# Fanaticism,

leads the militants to blind themselves
to the lack of democracy from the leaders
of the party,
to the fanatics not to forgive managers' errors
or not to recognize the good moves
of the other team,
to the religious to believe that
God is only on the walls of the church,
to the indebted who cling to the hope of the lottery
and to the scarce capacity to think, to lose faith
and not to believe in themselves.
Fanaticism is a very dangerous vice with
which we should not be involved.

# Why do we call crazy those who are different?

Why do we insist on not recognizing that others
have qualities that are superiors to ours?
Shouldn't we open our mouths to talk about
someone only if we're going to praise him/her?
An effort to focus on processes
and not on people will always add more value,
and clearly, better results.

# Civility is like daylight,

we can live without it,
but everything is more tumultuous
when it is missing.
Could you live in civility,
respecting the rules of coexistence,
such as walking through the established areas,
complying with the rules of transit,
giving everyone equal opportunity
and applying sanctions to the rapists,
to the irresponsible,
and so avoiding the permissibility?

# True happiness

and the path to the development of a nation
begin with the respect for the right of others.

It's not the clothes he/she
is wearing nor is the perfume.
It's not the vehicle from which he/she gets out
nor is it the money in his/her pocket.
It is with the quality of action
and with the content of what has been said
how the value of the work must be decided
as well as the respect to be deserved.

# When we judge people

just by their appearance,
we run the risk of supporting deception.

# It is not the same

to look for someone to blame than to be guilty,
but sometimes we put so much effort
into attributing to others our own mistakes
that we wear out mercilessly.

If you presume of what you do not practice,
you will end up showing recklessly

everything you lack.

# Blessed are those

who hear the sounds since
that means they are able to hear.
And if they hear,
they are in a position to explain why,
knowing everything they hear,
they do not contribute to the elimination
of pronounced evils before they are executed.
Or is the phrase,
"silence means consent" a lie?

If you have a bale of evidence,
then why do you intend to win the battle in front
of the public and not in front of the judge?
When you presume that you are innocent,
you just have to prove it,

# not blackmailing others.

# A mind

pregnant with unconformity
only generates discomfort, errors,
and more unconformity. An empty,
unsubstantial mind produces nothing,
but it is more susceptible to being filled
with viruses and debris
because it is easier for a weak person
to be influenced by what is harmful.
A person who does not devote enough time
to the art of good thinking,
ends up acting foolishly and thus,
with wrong results.

# There are people

who are only good for writing speeches
and there are very competitive people
who are very good at making them.
These are people who,
if they were to move out of their comfort zone
would become perfect losers.
I do not understand then,
why they do not devote themselves
solely to their specialties,
instead of being involved in everything,
without caring for the requirements or competencies
to have a good performance and,
therefore, look for what could be of benefit
for the majority.

# Watch out

out for those who play all the bases,
the ones who can do "whatever".
These experts in nothing and specialists i
n everything usually are rich in weaknesses
and when they want to correct them,
the effect is the opposite,
and they end up with thicker weaknesses.
If you happen to be like this,

## revise yourself!

**209**

There are people
who always go with the flow.
They only move in the direction of the wind
and for nothing in the world,
take the risk of going the opposite way.
They are people who arrive where the forces
of the wind take them,
not where they decide to be.

# A life like that

is too simple
and scarce of challenges.
God forbids that I become that way too.

Can a judge be fair if he/she is biased
or if he/she hasn't studied the case well,
or if beforehand,
he/she has the belief that the prosecutor
does everything wrong,
or if the verdict is based on what the press says,
or by following political instructions,
or judging by the way the defendant dresses
or speaks or by the defendant's skin color?

# Never judge

unless you are free of sin.

It is beautiful to get anywhere,
to have whom to call
and with whom to share stories and goals.
It is a wonderful spectacle
that someone looks for you, and says:
You are my brother and I love you"
or that when sadness and despondency get to you,
that someone also gives you a hand,
gives you a smile, pats you on the back
and hugs you, with an invitation to begin anew.

# What a privilege!

When they come and they open the windows,
they clean the soul with you;
they take out a piece of bread
without you knowing how
and show you that there is life beyond all possibilities.
Those are the true friends.

# Long live true friends,

now and forever!

There are people who seek higher social status
by breaking away from those who always
supported and defended them.
They do not realize that the desires for growth
are dwarfed when the virtue of gratitude is lost
and when we marginalize the fundamental allies.

There is no

# individual achievement

that has not counted with support
from other people; there is no victory alone.
That only exists in some card games
and I believe that not even there.

# Do not give prizes

to those who have not won the lottery,
or to those who have not done
something that deserves a gift,
gratification or special recognition.
No incentive should be free,
no matter how good-natured you are.
If you do, you encourage inertia,
irresponsibility and overprotective paternalism.
When you're going to give something
make sure that who receives it
is always the one that contributes the most ideas,
makes the bigger effort, is very reliable,
is easy to deal with, delivers good results
and shows the willingness
to have the job well done.

**214**

Are you a judge, prosecutor,
defendant, plaintiff, lawyer, journalist
or part of the public?
What role do you have in court?
Forgetting the role that one plays
by pretending to play the role of another person,
without having won it, is irresponsible and probably,
you will make serious mistakes.
Always seek to play the role pertaining to you
and grow from it, letting others fulfill theirs.
If you want to play another role,

# you have every right

to do so,
but first you have to conquer it.

If you cry when you cut onions,
it is because you have not learned
how far to extend your arms
and place the bulb at the right distance
when cutting them.
If you cut a finger during the preparation of meat,
it may be because you were not fully concentrated
in what you were doing.
If you spill the water from the bucket
used for cleaning,
it is because you did something wrong.

# There's no chance,

everything has a why.
In kitchen work like in any other activity,
if you know what you are doing thoroughly,
your chances of success are greater.
When you do not,
it's best to ask and proceed carefully.

# It's not the same thing

to be a clown than to do antics.
The clown is supposed to be a professional
who delights the public with his/her act
for which she/ he lives creating and practicing,
so that her/his act is dynamic
and different each time.
Instead, someone who makes antics
without being a professional clown
often becomes ridiculous and is mocked
by those she/he tries to conquer.

**217**

# Don't be late,

don't leave anyone waiting for you
beyond the time you promised to be there.
Do not waste other people's time by talking
or doing things for which
they were not summoned up and,
if you are going to give an excuse,
ensure that it is real and valid.

The time of others is not yours,
respecting it is an obligation.

# Farmers know

when to start mowing,
when to plow,
when to sow the seeds
and when to irrigate the plants
to have a good harvest.
That process properly done ensures
a fertile land to be really productive.
To have good soil is not enough;
it is essential to cultivate it well
and to take good care of it.
If you apply this peasant's rule
to whatever action you undertake,
your chances of success will be very advantageous.
If you do not know the terrain
where you are going to move to
and you do not know what it is good for,
watch out!
You can be stepping on quicksand.

**219**

If we are all in a certain place at the same time,
why can some people see things that others,
from the same place or position do not see
and if they see them,
they do not understand what they see?
The mechanics is not just to look toward
the same direction as others;
a sense of attention and a tuning of
your senses should also be developed.
The person who does not develop
a sense for the invisible,
or for observing more carefully
and for listening to the inaudible,
does not see beyond his nose,
does not feel and

# does not understand.

Selling peanuts in the streets,
throwing malicious innuendos and

# telling lies,

almost always leads to the same place: to poverty.
The only difference is that in the first case,
it is economic poverty
and in the second case it is mental poverty.
Remember,
regularly the first is product of the second
and the second can generate the first.

# The power of giving

means that whatever you receive or obtain,
you must share a percentage with those in need.
I'm not talking about giving alms to a beggar,
but about income distribution.
The more you give the more you receive.

# It is not wise

to hide our mistakes,
imputing falseness to others,
pretending ourselves to be clean.
Permanent success begins
with being ethical and recognizing your faults.

# Hope

is the energy pro resilience of the needy;
it is a push to the side of the possibilities
and should be the focus of practices of efficiency
and effectiveness.
Hope is not to stop, it is to persist;
it is not to sit and wait, it is to go out and search;
it is not the impossible,
it is the feeling of creativity and achievement;
it is not sitting on your hands,
it is betting on the outcome
of the continuous process to reach your goals.

# Don't give up

when things get tough.

It is at that time when you must show your worth
and be resilient in thought and work.
The best chances of success come
when you face difficulties.

# What happens

when you don't do anything?

What do you get when you stay static?
How does it affect you to be quiet
when everyone needs your opinion?
Doing nothing is the same
as not getting anything, as not producing,
as living without living.
If that's what you think you were made for,
you have serious problems with yourself.
No one is called to the ineffectiveness.
You came to the world for a reason
that of course, is not that of uselessness.
Therefore, when you feel
that you have lost the desire to create,
to think or to produce, liven up,
shake off, move, recycle your brain,
But never let the possibilities of creation
and production go without you.

# Let your son

exploit his own convictions,
to ripen his own fruits, to use his hands
and not yours to do his work
so that he knows what it costs to finish it.
If you want to have a being with thoughts,
words and performances like yours,
then become a clone,
and let your son mold his own shell.
He needs to understand and learn to manage
himself in a world that,
although it seems like yours,
will never be equal to yours.
Of course, he will need your leverage,
your push and your tracking for him to take off,
but if he must carry your weight to fly,
he might end up with a forced landing.

# Before

singing in public,
practice a lot and consult with an expert.
It is not the same to sing in the bathroom
or in the courtyard, than to face the public.
You must be aware
and not involve yourself in actions
in which you cannot guarantee
a good performance.

# What if you get kicked?

Take advantage of that
push forward and keep walking!
Life sometimes expresses hardness
just so that you advance into higher stages.

# The decision

of thinking before acting
is the key to avoid difficult situations.
Many situations would be avoided if,
before acting, we stop to meditate
and then decide the course of action;
although it is good sometimes,
but only sometimes, to let improvisation
and daring decide your next move.

There are lots of examples of prisoners
or inmates who, after being released from prison,
have preferred to return to jail.
For them,

# "freedom"

in the outside
is worse than confinement in prison;
It should be nonsense.
The real thing is that
when we do not respect the right of others
to live in freedom,
we are turning the natural space
into a prison.

# It is not surprising that

there are corrupt people and corruptors.
What would be surprisingly sad is
that you suddenly discover
that someone in your environment
has fallen into that abjection.

# Gossiping is a sickness,

an addiction or a bad skill.
Whatever its characterization,
it is harmful to those who practice it,
and for those to whom it is directed.
We must isolate the gossip
and especially the gossipy people.

# A good profit

should always go to the persevering
and thankful people who do not try to take
what is not rightfully theirs.

# When you go on flying high,

you fly swiftly among the clouds.
It's as if the sky was down below you.
Feelings of grandeur happen incessantly
and it seems that only you reign,
but it would be a real disaster
to forget that you will soon land.

# We need

to use a bit more the best of our abilities:
think before you act.
Isn't it simple?

# Does your tongue know

how to use words intelligently
so that they add value to you,
instead of difficulties?

It is said that the tongue
is the punishment of the body;
That's why you have to always train it
in the good use of the language.
To do so, your mind and your heart
must be coordinated with good,
collaboration and success.
Then you will need neither to curse nor to violate,
but to tell the truth responsibly.

# The word nonsense

means action or comment lacking reason,
foundation or logic.
When you make a foolish decision,
product of the effervescence of the moment,
without investigating,
or thinking well before acting,
you could be jeopardizing your future
and that of the people with whom you are involved,
or on whom you exert influence.

# Action

# The challenge

is to put into practice
what you learned and get results,
not to pass the test.

**239**

# Knowing

when
to shut up
is added value.
To say what we cannot sustain
could lead us to support, even indirectly,
whom we should never recognize.

You are a being of a superior nature.
To accomplish great achievements,
which could transform
and allow a more effective and dignified habitat,
is not a misuse of efforts for others to enjoy but, an
unavoidable responsibility
that you must assume.
Maybe you have already wasted
quite a bit of whatever resources
you had to invest in this mission,
but life always gives an opportunity
to those who review and redeem themselves
by taking their assigned road
and leaving a positive legacy.
Remember that your deadline gets closer
as each second goes by.
The moment to turn around and start over is

# NOW.

# Practice

with
your children
the things they like doing
if you want to achieve the power
to conquer their hearts
and be taken into account.
Everything begins with the development
of the capacity to combine your interests
with the interests of others,
especially with your people,
because you develop respect,
understanding, leadership and power of orientation.
The relationship between you
and the children is a great school,
for as long as you direct it
as if you were a coach and not a provost.

# Do not aspire

to positions,
privileges or conditions
that have been established for all
by the universal principle of equal opportunity.
Do not kick the one who serves you
or condition the decisions of others
for your own benefit.
Do not go down before the bus stops
or pretend the seat that does not belong to you.
It goes easy and falls into discredit
what is achieved without merit.

# I have knowledge

that I can teach,
but there are many more that I must learn
or unlearn. I always pray to have enough humility
and conviction to know how to distinguish them
from each other.

I'm going to put on a muzzle
so I don't have to bite the bricks of hope.

# That is to say,

to ensure that I could wait for the precise time
of things to happen and have faith to believe
in the actions that will fulfill every one of my dreams.

# Distrust,

just in case,
those who speak so much about their seriousness
that they even oppose being reviewed.
Or do you need to prove vociferously
what only needs concrete, visible,
documented and verifiable facts?

## Huh?

It will always be possible to be more and give more,
to right the wrong, correct the errors, release the
moorings, pass the boundaries,
awaken in the arms of the aurora and

# live happily.

It always has to be possible to reach it.
It only depends on you, me and us all.

# Make

the best
investment in you.

First invest in the work that you are.
If your investment is insufficient,
without proper plans, values or controls,
you will not be able to achieve good results that can
be invested in your children, relatives,
other people or other businesses.

Love, live, throw, create, open, break, draw,

reach out, feel and laugh.

Enjoy, forgive, thank and laugh.

Extend, palpate, investigate, clarify,

precise and laugh.

Eat, exercise, listen, ask, give, sing, dance, dare, pull,
look, advance, stop, push, go out,

free yourself and laugh.

Conquest, learn, express yourself,
teach, radiate, love, synchronize yourself,

search, deliver, laugh;

never stop dreaming and believing.
And if you have to mourn let it be of joy.
Let everything be for the well-being, prosperity,
and happiness for you and yours.

## Amen.

When you are on the edge of the cliff,
the decision you should make
is not to throw yourself into the void
to fall flat on your face,
but to grow wings on your sides
and fly to that dreamed place.

# ¡Never give up!

# To stop on time,

a fundamental condition to be happy.
To live a life like a car without brakes,
without paying attention to the stop signs
and without taking into account the others,
is to advance the arrival of the cliff and,
consequently, the disaster.

**251**

I'm going to build a village up in the air
to send all those people who always
want to live up there and never land.
Anyways,
as it is now "in", "living in the clouds",
we take away the problem
and see if they learn,
or maybe one of these days,
we just click on:

# "DELETE".

How great is the power to better oneself!

The more you forge it in your mind,
the more transcending the actions you make
and the more meaningful the achievements.

# Even more,

your quality to be an example
and a guide
will exceed your own goals.

# Your knowledge,

should be made available to the majority.
Knowledge is worthless if not shared
or if it is only used for personal glory.
The true taste of life occurs
when others grow with your growth
and vice versa.
Let your knowledge be distributed
and allow everything to flow.
You will see the great exchange of wisdom
that it generates.

# Give all people a chance,

even to those who seem not to deserve it.
But when someone has already shown,
even with the teachings,
not to have the attitude to do things right,
it is time to change to someone else.

# The sun

makes things that no other star can change.
Be like the Sun: come closer to what you want,
or do like the sea that never stops bathing the sand
which is always waiting for its waters.

# I know

that you are not happy
because you no longer speak with life
but with tastes and these are always momentary.
I know you're not happy because
you do not get impressed by anything
and you accept everything.
I know you're not happy
because you've tied yourself to the economy,
instead of working for the big dreams.
I know that you are not happy because
you have stopped believing in your own means and
you settle for the decisions of others.
I know you're not happy because
now you're a conformist without any aspirations.
I know you are not happy
because you laugh very little;
you do not shout your emotions and you do not talk
about purposes, but inertia.
Fortunately, I hope that since you have a brain and a
heart, one day you will want to start over.
Then, probably,
I'll be there to help you push your dreams,
from that side of thinking to this side of reality.

**2 5 7**

To fly over the swamps,
to pass the boundaries of ignorance,
to give image to values, to redesign habits
based on new truths
and to constitute in present the future.
I'm pursuing that now...

## ... and you?

# I let my anger go

and became a thinking person;
I let my tears go and gained my smile back;
I set the dogs free
and their barks frightened the nostalgia.
Now the only thing missing is a ceaseless rain
with the power to generate stray rivers
to sweep the paternalistic complaints
and the nefarious traps of lobbyists,
taking poverty to the swamp
and leaving the spaces opened to purification
and to the institutional sense.
I'm putting my share, do you?

# Make

your activities constant, productive,
cheerful, frank and shared.
Thus, you will have the best
excuse for the prevention of Alzheimer's,
monotony and bitterness.

# Go with my flow

and you'll get where I want you to be.
Decide your reach, set your route;
if necessary go against the flow.
Create your own paths
and you will arrive wherever you want to be.

# Always bet on

decisive and persistent people.
These, even if they have difficult times,
will always be ready to start over
until they achieve their goal.

**262**

# Thank God,

I do not have to worry
about going in the executive class
since I am superior and I travel in the main cabin.
Besides, the problem is not so much the class
in which you travel, but who you are with,
what results you get and what their use is.
No matter where you are,
act as the best do.

# If you hear

the river roaring
and the devouring noise that is coming swiftly
through its natural course,
run at full speed to a safe area and,
at the same time,
shout to others
so they too look to save themselves.

When you're in the forbidden zone,
you must be more agile than the river.
Otherwise,
if you are not liquidated by the stones, you will be
drowned by its waters.

# Social responsibility

is not, nor can it be to give alms, but a path capable
of connecting to other paths,
destined to the well-being
and progress of people
and have the following multiplier factors:

1. What you receive, you must share.
2. What you learn, you must teach.

**265**

# And if you lose ...

analyze the defeat, but don't stay in it.
Go back to your previous position,
take a deep breath, focus on the target,
lean in your strengths and start over.
Every day is a beautiful way to push
and bet on success until you succeed.

# Every now and then,

all of us do antics and laugh at them,
but turning the antics into a routine
creates the habit of being a clown.
In that case,
our permanent place must be
where our services as a clown are required,
not in those places where being a clown
is simply making a fool of us.

# Be careful

on barking when there is no danger
that deserves it,
you could be scaring friends,
co-workers and your own family.
And if you make barking a routine,
you'll terrorize even your own shadow.

# There are decisions

that are very heavy emotionally.
They are so heavy that the action of making them
costs a lot of effort, pain, tears, time and money.
However, you will never know for certain
what a heavy decision can bring you
until you make it.

**269**

# The suitcase

was made to carry the necessary stuff
for the trip you are going to undertake.
A suitcase with useless load means overweight,
discomfort for its transportation
and the threat of losing pieces.
Many times we cannot know it ahead of time,
but the heaviest thing in a suitcase
is not necessary:
Hate, gossip, grudges and pitfalls.

Please leave them out of your suitcase
and out of your heart before starting the trip.

# Do not stop

the one who wants to leave you,
or the one that does not want to be close to you
or who does not want to be under your care.
Ignore the unpleasant ones,
those who use profane words
and make disrespectful gestures.
Erase the one that keep an irresponsible
social page with no values.
Say NO to wastefulness,
constant exaggeration and inertia.
Never stop laughing or loving

... and if you cry, let the reason be worth the tears.

# Don't fear storms,

they'll always come.
What you really need to be afraid
of is your inability to face them.

When the trail runs out of exits,

## don't stop.

Keep on going, push the forest,
build other exits and mark them well
so that they could be found
by those coming behind you.

# There is a stain

that not even the best dermatologists,
manage to erase from the body of the wearer:
the stain of the embezzlement.
Please do not accept even a small splash of it.

# Pick up the mess.

Why collide so many times with the same piece
and not put it aside?
Is it worth living in chaos when a broom,
a garbage can, some water
and some of your time
can improve environmental conditions,
help organize furniture, eliminate dust
and allow clean air to penetrate
the corners of your home, your office
or any other place where you usually stay?
Nothing is better for optimism
than a nice atmosphere.

Let no one be taken by the recklessness,
the dishonest, or the vain pride!
Let no one lose the love
for the support to those in need
and do not let despair take over
because we have defined success with joy
and life with strong moral values.
And if we are surprised by death,
let it be to fertilize the smile,

# to be born again

and do with love better things.

# Do not live in flattery

nor give merit to people who you know,
have none.
Those orchestrators of words
are indecent people who live with the wicked purpose
of marketing with ragamuffins
and to grant them absolutely undeserved rungs
or conceits, obtained by means of traps.

I'm going to gather firewood
and ignite a stove to burn in
their embers the weeds of fear,
any stormy past and all knowledge without validity.

# Afterwards,

I'll soften in the flames any hardness
of my behavior to relax attitudes,
to give more of me
and to broaden the possibilities of collaboration
between me and those around me.

Do not let the pain stay forever,
nor allow the indecent people to infect you
with their bad behavior,
neither flatter the lying promises,
or look for applause
by appealing to others' ignorance.

# ¡No and no!

You're not like that.
Let them be!
Always the same ones,
the true pagans, the philosophers of deceit.
But not you, you belong in another category,
the one at the service of good
and that preaches with examples.

# Have respect

for those who have earned it
and submit those who have not
to all the considerations that apply.
If you understand it that way,
allow them to defend themselves.

You do not have to forgive
or cover the bad deed,
but you must avoid acting as a judge,
assessing everything by hearsay or instinctively,
without exhausting due process,
or without having evidence of the wrongdoings
someone has committed.

**280**

If you're going to dance to someone else's party,
make sure you've really been invited.
Once there,

# avoid getting drunk

whether there are reasons for it or not,
do not bump against the crockery,
do not fall in love with the owners of the house,
and least of all do not be the last one to leave.
There are drinks that it is better not to take
and places where it is absolutely required
to be well-behaved.

**2 8 1**

If you have one banana left,
give it to whoever needs it;

# maybe tomorrow

that person will bring you the glass of water you
need to quench your thirst.
If you let the banana go bad
instead of giving it to someone,
you will never know the value
that another person would give to your gift.

**282**

# Do good, anyways.

At the end,
whatever happens,
you'll always have the honor
that even the enemy will take off its hat
to recognize you and also,
the victories will continuously repeat.

**2 8 3**

If the allowance is only enough for "rice with eggs"
be satisfied with your lunch and,

# with a motivating smile,

get yourself ready to create the times of
"steaks and fish".

# Don't forget.

Before giving an opinion
know all the versions of those involved
in the issue or problem.
Decisions or recommendations are very biased
when we only have half truths,
or when information is conditioned
against favorite culprits.

# If suddenly

you get into a swamp and
feel that you will not be able to get out of there,
before crying or lamenting,
check how deep the space is next door.
Maybe it's not so deep
and you can free yourself with little effort.
There are swamps as deep as your mental capacity
to schedule and go for the exit.

**286**

He complains about the bed he sleeps on,
the laughter of his children, the food,
and about the people on the street.
He complains about the government
and the neighbor, the lottery he didn't win,
and the money he earned.
He complains about his breathing and the sun.
It is better to give the cold shoulder
to that perennial whiny, to get away from him,
because he only generates negative energies
and that's not what you want for you,

## or is it?

# If the road
# gets tough

and your strength gives in,
look for a shade and rest.
Ask for help to generate new energies
and if necessary, check the travel plan
and adjust it to the new circumstances.
If you have to change route don't be afraid,
but never forget the goal.
Your sense of success is to reach it.

# ¡Have fun!

Explore the unknown.
Let your mind and body
penetrate into unaccustomed areas.
Go for what's different, appreciate every detail;
smile for all the nice things you find,
touch what attracts you and close your eyes
to fill yourself with its variations and textures.
Inhale the aromas, distinguish them,
taste the flavors of everything as much as possible
and give thanks all the time.
Let life express itself openly
and relaxed through you.

# Scream out of joy,

celebrate every achievement,
every conquest, every new opening.
Let your laughter impact your whole body
and fill your spaces with vitality
whenever you get good results.
Life and happiness are prolonged
when you have the opportunity to commemorate
the fulfillment of your goals.
The more you celebrate success,
the more reasons you will have to celebrate again.

Don't forget to be thankful for every achievement.

At least once a week
try to have something to celebrate,
for whom to toast, whom to recognize.

# When you celebrate,

you make it clear in your mind
that you are a successful person,
capable of reaching goals, making dreams come true.
In addition,
you will find more allies
willing to share your achievements.

How many books have you read?
Which ones?
Actually, that doesn't matter.
Where you are now is the result of your decisions,
your readings and general actions.
However, the books you read from now on
could contribute significantly
in giving a twist to your life and your results.

# It's up to you.

**2 9 2**

Do you commit to something and don't deliver?
Are you a responsible person,

# yes or no?

All broken promises are based on irresponsibility,
in committing to what cannot be fulfilled,
in violating the agreements.
If you want to be a unifying factor
rather than a conflicting one,
start by complying with the agreements
and make sure you make the rules clear
before committing.

# We are

the choices we make every day.
That is why it is of primary importance
to be careful when in despair.
When we make decisions and act out of despair,
there is a very high probability of total failure.
No matter how urgent things seem to be,
stop for a moment, integrate all the information
and meditate on the details
before deciding or choosing an option;
it will always be worthwhile.
You can afford to improvise only in those times
when you want to venture
and you are completely sure of the result.

**2 9 4**

Nothing like being thankful,
enjoying who you are and how you are.
Gratitude solidifies love,
recognizes and highlights the contributions of others
and places you as a special human
and spiritual being.
Thank then your God, nature,
all of those who have put something in you and also
those who always smile at you,
or provide you warmth or with a service.
Be thankful to yourself for everything and,
above all, for having the quality

# to recognize
# the actions of others.

Ask all the questions that need to be asked

# No one fails for asking

and no one errs by asking for clarification
of what he/she has not understood.

If you get to overcome your own demons,
you will be ready to face any problems
that arise in your life.

# Learn,

liberate and strengthen your mind;
demons are not invincible.

Things need to be well done
from the very first moment.
It doesn't matter who you do them for.
If you decided to do something,
make sure you are committed with its planning
and execution, with the highest level of security
and perfection.
Do not stop honoring your work and commitments,
because afterwards,
the risk will be very high and

# losses can
# become unbearable.

# If fear

prevents you from doing what you have always
dreamed of, you have two choices:
to forget about your dreams
or to overcome your fear.
The truth is that no fear is so powerful
that it cannot be eliminated.

Jesus
resurrected and you too can be born again
based on ethical behavior, respect
and love for the others, by changing your habits,
unlearning what does not work, learning new skills,
assuming your commitments
and giving more to your community.

# Renew yourself
# every day!

And do your part for a happy world

**300**

# Give credit
# to those that deserve it.

Don't let ambition and selfishness
make you fall into the trap of discredit.
When you try to cover up the merits of others
you affect to your own growth.

# Always honor yourself,

by achieving your promotion in any group
or organization in which you participate,
based on merits and
not by assignment or imposition.

# Say NO!

to excess in all situations.
Be demurred even when being grateful.
Exaggeration is superfluous,
annoying and can cause damage
99.9% of the times.

# Sometimes,

you get so wrapped up in a habit
that it becomes impossible to appreciate
how little it brings you for you to continue in it.
Therefore, it is imperative to periodically do the task
of revising, updating and changing your habits.

Is it writing poetry the concatenation of words
that intertwine to the contagious rhythm
of fragrances and attuned to the senses?
Is it an ideology to cross the abyss of illusions
and create bridges that allow the transfer of ideas?
Is it a victory to expose the dreams with results
and ignite the celebrations with them?
Is it enjoying life to reject the tales of bad omens, to
drive away with strong winds
the harmful people around you,
to let aside the insecure
and not to allow joy to die?

It does not matter what the answers are.
The key thing is that if you want fragrance, harmony,
poetry, bridges, own ideas, respect for your ideology,
to live the dreams, to celebrate, to reach your goal,
positive mental attitude, joy and full life;

# you must act
# to have them.

It all starts with you; look inside.

# In the course of time

life puts you through tests and more tests.
Approving them will depend on how clear
you have your objectives,
as well as your values and principles.
The power of the approach
means concentrating on the goal
and not distracting yourself
with unimportant matters,
nor with the superficial,
nor with anything
that does not correspond with your purposes.
If you have many open fronts
and you treat them all with the same priority,
it is very likely that none will be properly concluded
and your failure will be resounding.

The long wait is gone
and I stayed without doing what I always wanted.

# Has this happened to you?

Did you ever wait so long to take a step
that time got tired of waiting for you?
Now you have a new chance,
will you still take a long time
or will you take a step right away?
The willingness to start on time
usually transforms everything.
You immediately realize how positive
currents move in your favor.
Don't wait any longer,
Now is the time!

# It is not always worthwhile

to say what you think.
Sometimes it is better to shut up
until the scandal is over,
wait for the other to express her/himself
to ensure your understanding of the messages.
When the adrenaline level has risen so much
that it seems as if you were fighting,
when you notice that nobody is listening to you,
when you do not interpret what you are saying,
when you repeat what you said before
and feel that you will offend,
it is better to shut up.
It is not always worthwhile to talk.

It is more difficult a
nd requires doubling your effort to do
what is more complicated,
but its benefits can last a lifetime.
When you face the big problems assigning them
a higher priority, the small ones are not even noticed.
As Covey would say:

# "first things first".

309

Adjust your temperature

# tune in with
# the good vibe

and your emotional intelligence
will always avoid unpleasant situations.
Remember that high temperatures
are causes of heart attacks.
Learning to control emotions is very rewarding
and its positive effect lasts forever.

# Live your decisions,

be responsible for them
and give a complete follow-up to their details
and processes. Enjoy their implementation
and your achievements to the maximum,
but if for some reason, the process is not working,
recognize it promptly, correct it, change your decision
or simply remove it forever.
Do not persist in doing something whose evaluation
tells you that you will not get anywhere.

**311**

# Take at least one day of each month

and devote it to improve your community,
whether participating in a professional
or community organization,
dictating classes at a university,
collaborating with a cleaning day,
supporting the neighbor to solve a situation,
respecting the transit signals,
teaching your children to be better citizens,
not littering in the streets, etc.
Our actions of social responsibility
will always be a contribution to peace
in our society.

# To focus

on the main objective until reached
is the most important task..
Not straying into irrelevant details
and always making an extra effort,
pushing a little bit more;
that is how you get to be successful.

Does it seem a small thing to you
to be a slave of your own thoughts
or to allow that someone else
decides your behavior with her/his actions?
Or don't you do what you have always wanted to do
for fear of what people will say?
Drop those chains!
Free up your mind.

# Break away from harmful people

and gain life and joy,
for that is why we have been sent to this earth.

I know that you all know it:

# the more you run away,

the faster you find yourself facing reality.
Study every situation, every problem.
Leave aside the one who will in no way
contribute anything
or that does not have the possibility to grow,
but to those that do,
face them with fortitude
and the energy of a Titan.
When you act that way,
everything will be different
and meaningful help will abound.

**3 1 5**

# ¡Today is screaming day!

For the solidarity with the roses
and for the right to choose who to be with.
For the word and for the ability to think freely,
for dignity and for participation based on merits.
Today all women sing loudly
for life to be respected
and for love to prevail
through poetry and integration.

# Menpo,

the positive mind God, has been born.
He sustains his divinity in the idea that the more
open, humble, respectful of others, and more positive
your mind is, your possibility of turning your dreams
into reality will be much bigger.

# 317

# Learning never ends.

Don't try to put an end to it.
The best school is life itself.
There are those who pass through life
without graduating in any of the opportunities
it offers them every day.
Don't do the same.
Always check your agenda for the day,
the week or the month.
Evaluate the results;
take into account the mistakes
so not to make them again
or to make it a habit.
Prepare your new plan
for greater accomplishments.
That is what I call continuous learning.

# Dare!

Break the parameters,
get the dreams out of you
and put them to fly making them into realizations.
Bring down the drowsiness hand;
oxygenate your body by removing the oxide
from its inertia.
Do not wait any longer;
be yourself in the sense of change,
achievements and smiles.
There has been enough mourning already!

# Don't put limits
## on your aspirations,

your growth, or your life.
Even terminally ill people
can come back from death.
Everything is possible if you can believe it
and keep a positive mental attitude.
When you set limits you close doors
and build walls, which is against all freedom.

# Learn to read well.

A word or punctuation
not seen or not understood
can make you interpret what is not,
and if you understand what it is not,
you decide ineffectually.

# Wherever you are,

feel happy and grateful.
Show your best smile
and the best disposition to give and receive.
Sit in the front row and if any protocol prevents it,
take a seat in the one behind it
and act as if you belong there.
Live every moment as the best of your life and do
not allow anyone, no matter who she/he might be,
to change that feeling.

When you meet friends,
take advantage of that time for good vibes,
solidarity, recognition, good memories,
a toast to new times, hugs and gratitude.
Do not lose a moment "killing enemies",
fighting over trivialities or making fun of others.

# Moments with friends

are so special!
Why not invest them without waste?

# Integrity

is a diplomatic visa to any good place.
Always prefer to leave out of you those heavy
things that add nothing to your life,
but never go out without your integrity.
And if for some reason being trustworthy
creates you a problem, persists in your convictions.
It is an excellent reason to swim against the current.

**324**

# Fear is a vulgar cretin

that we should put in its place.
Sometimes it goes with us and, in that case,
it should serve us as a precaution;
but we must never adopt it or give it a permanent
welcome and we must send it into exile
with absolute determination at the first opportunity.

Develop your memory
so that you

# never forget
# to say thanks

and have the ability to compare before deciding.

How greatness is usually transitory!
especially when it arrives as a loan
or just for the season.
Make always sure to have your feet firmly
on the ground and, if you are in the clouds
or near them, do not forget that
at some point in time, the plane will land.
That is, be prepared at every moment to return
to the first rung
without your conscience punishing you,
or have your ego exploding

# after so much climbing.

# Do not fail

when you are the principal actor or the host.
Your punctuality,
performance or attention to the guests,
must be first level,
regardless of the resources available.
Therefore, make sure to study and practice your
characters or commitments well,
because the distinctive seal is expressed by giving the
best of us in what we do,
especially when it is about our specialty
or our chosen profession.

# Be sure to be a hook and not bait;

; inhalation and not exhalation;
a sigh and not martyrdom.
Always become a gaze, not blindness;
become joy, not sadness;
become color, not mourning;
be tongs, not blisters.
Let life always allow you to extend your hand
instead of punching with your fist.

It is never the same when you are absent
as to when you are present,

# but if you are present,

try to make your presence noticeable,
especially for how well you make others feel,
that way, you'll make sure that when you're away
your return is longed for.

# Everyday

I look for something to do
that can transform someone's life positively:
like hugging someone,
making someone smile,
looking into someone's eyes
and saying I love you,
put my stamp on something,
extend the hand, say yes or no,
cause the crying, listen,
or any other valuable detail for him or her.
I don't always achieve it,
but on countless occasions
I have received powerful and satisfying feedback.

**3 3 1**

# Praising the one who deserves it

is not only a way to motivate;
it's also a way of teaching quality behavior
during the job's daily routine,
And it is also a great way to ensure shared success.
I emphasize the importance of the merit of praise,
as well as giving it immediately;
it verifies the action of the collaborator,
not when the praised
doesn't remember why he receives it,
but at the moment of it happening.

# Don't give me any spilled food

if you don't want me to dirty your rug.
Don't promise me saddlebags
if you're never going to give them to me.
Do not swear by anyone other than yourself
or hand over resources to pay
for what you have not received.

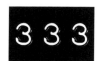

# There will always be someone in disagreement

with what you say or do.
You will always have people
declared as your enemies,
even if you think you have
done nothing to deserve it,
and it can always happen that your presence
is not pleasant for certain people.
If you concentrate on the actions of the rejecters,
you will never have the wonderful opportunity
to enjoy the real actors,
those who add value to your life
and add competitive advantages to your work.

# Check your closet frequently;

Something there might be in need of cleaning,
repairing or changing.
Check your pantry periodically,
some products may have already
past their expiration date
and cannot be used when required.
Keep track of your friends;
it may be that several of them
need a follow-up call,
a just-for-hugs visit or a reunion
to relive the good all times.
Review your followers on social networks,
maybe some deserve to be "deleted"
for having stopped living based on good principles
and better moral values.
Do not postpone the beginning of the project
that you have always wanted,
because time spent without any action, is a loss.

**335**

# Trust your potentials.

The first raw material to succeed
is to trust yourself.
All the great discoveries occurred
and continue to occur,
because the dreamer believed
he/she could and persevered
until completing the feat.
Don't forget to trust others either.
Their support will be the second ingredient that,
when mixed with your dreams,
can push you to glory.

**336**

Every difficult situation is an opportunity.
Every moment is the moment
and every place is a destiny.
The most important thing will always be
to connect your dreams to the realities of time
and space, and the gathering of the resources to
achieve it will immediately begin.

Don't waste time on disquisitions,
just focus on the goals and

# ACT!

# Surprise everyone

by being the way you are;
show up where no one is expecting you.
Dress your best and sneer at the problems
by coming up with effective solutions.
Give the best of you in every action
and infect each and every day those around you
with your positive mental attitude,
with your ability to get better results,
with your great ways to be cheerful
and with your availability to give love
without charging for it.

# Come on, you can do it!

# Be careful when talking.

Listen carefully
and shut up when someone else is talking;
ask if you didn't hear right or didn't understand.
Think and then answer firmly,
but also with respect
and without raising your voice
as if you were talking
with a sledgehammer in your mouth.

# Do not tie the rope so tight

that someone could fall;
also, do not make innuendoes
or write messages on the social media that
you dare not to say face to face.
Do not sharpen a pencil
without cleaning the garbage produced.

To always have clarity of action is a life standard
and your responsibility.

# Don't run

away from your shadow because,
even if it shrinks, fattens, enlarges
or hides behind you,
it'll never leave your side.

# Of course, miracles exist!

I have many results that show
the reality of miracles.
Do you want to try it?
Here I leave you an exercise:
stand in front of a mirror, the bigger the better.
Close your eyes and say:

## "I am a miracle."

Open your eyes
and look at the person on the other side,
aim with your index finger and say,
"I am a miracle, am I not?"
You'll be surprised at the answer.
Then go do your work
with the empowered mind
of the miracle that you are.
You'll be much more surprised.

# Enjoy

your dinner
as if it was your most precious conquest,
as if with it you were going to transform your life
and be everything you ever dreamed of.
Make from each flavor a delight
and from each sensation a gratitude
for the enormous privilege
of being able to celebrate with your dinner
the grace of life.
Put aside everything that does not do you well,
not just during that instant of gratitude,
but forever.

**343**

How many people will you be able to hug today,
smile at and say thank you?
So many people walk everywhere in need of a hug
that if you decide to hug those you could,
you would have received back smiles,
feelings of love, health improvement
and a sense of opportunity.
Since that feels so good,
I invite you from this moment on
to carry out the task of the hug,

# so that we all live more.

# Everything dries up,

even desire,
but to sow again
has to always be the goal
and the action to take
until everything turns green
and flourishes again.

How many of us may recognize
the messages of thunder?
These announce that some things will change
almost immediately and suddenly
... lightning, rain, torrents of water
flow through the streets
and people running to avoid getting wet!
The mind and the heart often act like thunder:
They send us messages
announcing changes and storms,
but we do not listen to them
and then situations happen
and we get drenched in problems
and conflicts that, for not being foreseen,
become very difficult for us to solve.

# Learn how to interpret your body's messages

and it will be easier for you to reach your goals.

# Express your smile today,

for the benefit of love and good living.
Please offer it to every person you come across to
or to whoever comes to see you.
Let's make a bunch of joy out of smiles
for others' hearts.

# Take this day

to grab a broom and sweep.
Clean from the heart
all that weights more than lead,
such as vain pride, insensibility, hate,
gossip and sadness.
Use it to sweep the lack of participation
in national affairs and corruption.

May this day be to begin again
and to be happier.

**348**

# Take every new day

to recreate your mind,
to start over, to fight boredom
and to say NO to routine.

Don't forget to hug and believe.

If someone feels offended by you
or thinks that you made a mistake,
have the humility to ask for forgiveness,
even if you know that your acting was correct
and the facts are being confused.

# Humility

will always be the difference
between getting ahead
and being caught up in defeat.

# Fulfilling your commitments

guarantees the success of the agreements
and reduces the likelihood of conflicts.

# If you're not happy

with who you are
remember that you are the result of your doings.
If you change your behavior,
you'll change what you are.

# Persist:

Perseverance is always accompanied
by tough battles,
but it leaves lasting
and greater satisfactions.

# Being punctual

is a sign of respect to others,
a guarantee for effective use of time
and a success factor for leadership.
Punctuality motivates confidence
and instills a responsible attitude in others.

# Take a good look

at those people who complain about everything;
they don't feel good about anything
and they always blame others for their problems.
You'll see that they have a lot of difficulties
getting ahead
and very limited support among the others.
In fact, complaining constantly
moves you away from the solutions
and pushes you to precipice.

# Be sympathetic to those in pain,

a companion in joy,
fair in the application of justice,
intransigent with dishonesty,
focused on the objective,
restrained in your spending,
humble in victory
and grateful to all your collaborators.

**356**

To live with a purpose always adds.
Sometimes it looks like it's all over, but it's just the
right time to take a leap forward.

# Don't stop ... go on!
# go on!

**357**

When you go to unravel the hank
make sure that the liberated part
does not get tangled again,
because then,
the mess will be greater than

# the solution you were looking for.

**358**

# Do not stop loving

just because someone makes different decisions
that go against your interests,
either by unusual impulses,
aggressive disagreements,
or because love bit on another hook.
To love without charging for it,
is to flow with the grace of life.

# Today, get out of

your dwelling
and explore the small details outside:
the sunrise, the tiny wild flowers,
the offers from the brunette who sells mangos,
the smile of a child crossing by your side
in the arms of his mother,
the cadence of a lady
who does not let you see her face,
the colors of the rainbow,
the greeting from the elderly man
and the shape of each house.
Life is made of beautiful details
that we almost never appreciate
in all of its dimensions.

# Laugh at sadness

and laugh at yourself.
Laugh at everything you imagine that implies joy.
Laughing is a space without waste that clears the
roads and gets the trauma out.
Forget the bitterness and

## celebrate the triumph!

**3 6 1**

If you get kicked, get up!

# Keep on going.

Don't lose the horizon of your goals,
but never allow to be kicked again.

**362**

# Remember

to make a checklist of your interior every day
just in case you lack important issues
to take into account: love to give,
purposes to reach, forgiveness to ask for or that,
on the contrary,
you have more than enough reasons to hate,
conflicts to forget,
regrets to erase and properties to return.

**363**

# Love and forgive

no matter the treachery,
the deceit or the ingratitude.
Devote yourself to do good anyway,
although all the good you do
is enjoyed by who does not deserve it.

# Celebrate every accomplishment,

every arrival and every delight.
Let your mind, your heart and all your body know
the successes you reach.
Celebrating is a very practical way to be happy,
to live longer and to show your worth.

# Today I just want to say thanks and apologize.

Thank you all from my natural mother to my foster mother, and even the last person I met yesterday. From my beloved father to my last great boss. From my daughter Jael to my grandson Dariel. From my childhood friends and for all the friends who have accompanied me through this journey of life to today's friends, full of emotions and eager for adventures. From my natural brothers to my brothers-friends. From the dreamed love to the virtues and later realities. From the small country to the great universe. From the knowledge of God to his eternity.

# Thank you, thank you and thank you.

And please, forgive me for my sins, for my mistakes and for many times looking at life in ways different than others see it. Sorry for not regretting anything and for putting aside things that affected or were of interest to many. Forgive me for being myself and for always looking for my own voice. For not fearing the future or death, for not seeking what others wanted, but to always live in my own way. Sorry for being indifferent or too fussy; for screwing over, for stopping to screw over and for believing that everyone can become what they dreamed of, even against the worst of difficulties. Forgive me for being open, and thank you for allowing me to be; after all, I've never wanted to be anything more than what I am today.

# One very important thing:

Every time I have been able to and wanted to, I have had good moments of happiness and I am clear that happiness is on its way, despite the bad omens of the time and the mouth of some "prophets". Every day you can and you must learn more and more. At the same time, we must remove what no longer serves us, not even for remembrance.

Learning does not occupy any space, but it opens spaces, and happiness is not only ageless, but also pure enjoyment.

I apologize to all of those I let down or I did not under-stand, or when "I acted like crazy", or when I showed that I got tired of being tired. Sorry for not even com-plaining when the pain seemed to obliterate my senses, or when the words from other mouths struck me so hard, that my heart fled out of cowardice. I have friends who are my brothers. I have brothers who are friends and letters of refuge. I have foster parents, people who came and went, people who left, but they didn't go. For all of them my gratitude. For my children, you know ... I have wanted to and I have not been able to, I have been able to and I have forgotten, I have done and has not turned out well, I have decided and it has not worked out, I have promised and I have not fulfilled.

Sometimes it seems that I am not around, sometimes it seems that I do not return; however my children, I've always tried and I'm going to keep on trying, I always love you. You are always first in my thoughts and I seek to make an investment in myself whose beneficiaries are you. That won't change with the years or with the different routes that I might take, or with the times. For all of you my respect, love and full disposition. May life continue to allow me to count on you always.

# ... so be it!

*Reflection-Reaction-Action:*
*365 Reflections for a Successful Living*

*Dominican Republic*
*2018*

94049148R00217

Made in the USA
Lexington, KY
22 July 2018